My Beloved Canadian Friends Sandy & Ricky —

Happy Cooking & Feasting.

Hopefully we may share some together down the years.

Love

Jayne xx

"Enjoy taking the time to create your own local food journeys, turn over your own culinary stones and discover what your local community has to offer."

www.freshalicious.ca

Acknowledgements

Steve—Thanks for always being there and putting up with my long hours. You have supported me and believed in me all the way. **Anastasia, and Nicoletta**—Thank you girls for always being so good and supporting the cookbook. You have both been a really great inspiration for me to open up and share our lives, recipes and way of life knowing we can help others. I love you both incredibly. **Mom**— thanks for your love and support, always. Your complete confidence in me gives me the strength to take on the most challenging feats, and succeed. And let's not forget, thanks for the dishes I borrowed to get me started. Love you lots. **Dad**— thanks for teaching me respect for the land we live on at a very early age. You were probably one of the first real recyclers of just about anything next to grandma. As well, thanks for all those camping tips and cooking over an open fire, my memories are fond and unforgettable. **Anna**—Thanks for the advice in the kitchen over the years and sharing your love of really great Greek food. You have contributed greatly to my culinary education, and that I am forever thankful. Efaristo Yaya! **Tom**— thanks for sharing your culinary secrets and your knowledge behind great food. Working in the restaurant with you has definitely given me a wealth of knowledge for what makes people happy. Efaristo Papou! **Grandma**, it has been a while since your passing, and not a week passes without remembering your visits to my apartment to teach me how to cook really fantastic Ukrainian food, never mind the traditional secrets passed down to me. Everytime I cook I remember you. **Kim**—you will be greatly missed, with love for your family, Morgan and you children.

With love, Stacey

To all my friends (you all know who you are), thanks for sharing wonderful moments with Steve and I, and supporting me and the ***Freshalicious™*** cookbook project. May fresh local and healthy be the pinnacle of your lives.

www.freshalicious.ca

Recipes © Stacey Fokas
Food Stylist Stacey Fokas
Lifestyle Text Stacey Fokas
Contributing Design by Stephen Owen
Wine Notes by Hugh Sutherland

Photography © Mike McColl: 29,67,71,79,81,91,105,109,149,153,169,181,189,213,255,273,303,305,331,347,355
Photography © Lisa Clements: 49,61,69(l,c),77,95,113,131(l)141,151(l),211,239,275,301(lrg,l,r),341(t),363
Photography © Simon Burn: front cover: 5,13,21,25,27,31,33,35,37,39,41,43,45,47,51,53,55,57,59,63,65,69(t,b),73,75,83,85,87,89, 93,97,99,101,103,107,111,115,117,119,121,123,125,127,129,131(s),133,135,137,139,143,145,147,151(s),155,157,159,161,163,165,167, 171,173,175,177,179,183,187,190,191,193,195,197,199,201,203,205,207,208,209,214,215,216,217,219,221,223,225,227,229,231,233, 235,237,241,243,245,247,249,251,253,257,259,261,263,265,267,269,271,277,279,280,281,283,285,287,289,291,292,293,295,297,299,30 1(s/c),307,309,311,313,315,317,319,321,323,325,327,329,333,335,337,339,341(b),343,345,349,351,353,357,359,365

Published in Canada by **InFokas Productions**. ISBN 978-0-9866308-0-4 Printed in USA.
Creative direction and design by Stacey Fokas.
First Edition.

Acknowledgements

Photography by: Mike McColl, Lisa Clements & Simon Burn

Steve Fokas, *Cowhide Promotional Wear Inc.*—Thanks for allowing me to take on such a large project, and keeping everything together. Your contirbutions are greatly appreciated. **Stephen Owen**, *Resonate Creative*—without you, the ***freshalicious™*** cookbook would not have been completed. Your creative contibutions have been greatly appreciated. You saw my vision and helped me bring it alive, and that I thank you for. I want to thank **Simon Burn,** *SDB Creative* for his beautiful photography. **Marie Austin,** *Editor*—your friendship and support will always be in my heart and final touches on the book are greatly appreciated, thanks M. **Mark Pavilons**, *Editor,*—your contributions are greatly appreciated. **Sally Morrell**, *proof reader*—thanks for all your hard work.You have contributed in a heart-felt way and I truly appreciate your honesty and integrity. I look forward to the next book project. **Liz Shaughnessy**, *Liz Shaughnessy and Assoc.*—thanks so very much for helping me in ways that no one else can. Looking forward to the fun to come! **Boris Polakow**—for all the years we worked together, you have taught me how to be strong, persevere and that anything is possible! For this I am forever grateful. I was able to work with your visions, which in turn has greatly contributed to me building my own.Thank you. **Chef Ted Reader**, *BBQ King*—what can I say? You helped me when I needed it most, this cookbook is all that much better because of you. Wishing you all the best for your next great cookbook! **Mike McColl**, *Photos with Sauce*—thanks for helping me complete the book; your food photography is unsurpassed. The next cookbook will be all you, from start to finish! **Lisa and Corey Clements**, *Ravens Ridge Photography*—you are both wonderful to work with and I am extremely happy with your work. I am looking forward to working with you on the next project! **Jessica Bartelt**, *makeup artist*—thanks for the makep tips and your help on the project. **Maja Kolnic**, *hair stylist*—thanks for the great hair! **Annabel Andrion Barrozo,** *Food Preparation*—what can I say? You know how fond I am of you and all your contributions. You are truly wonderful - love ya lots! **Piero and Rose Carbone**, *Garden Foods*—thank you for all your support with the book and other projects we have worked on together. You are both wonderful, hard working people that contribute to our wonderful community. Caledon would not be the same without you both. **Mike Aballe**, *Concord Foods*—your support for my project does not go unnoticed. Thanks for everything! **Logan St. Clair**, *Apple Store, Sherway Gardens*—thanks for helping me out with my first Mac. What an incredible machine. Your assistance was greatly appreciated. **Steven Freiria**, *Chapters, Brampton, ON* —thanks for all your support and great advice for this book. It was greatly appreciated. I can't wait to see if I can fill all the stores with my book. **Michèle Bosc**, *Château des Charmes*—thanks for sharing your winery with me and taking on a portion of the wine pairing. Your contributions to the **freshalicious™** cookbook are greatly appreciated. **Tom Moyer**, *Cherry Avenue Farms*—thanks for sharing your wonderful farm with me so that I may share it with others. Wishing you much success for another 200 years. **Andrew Kohnen and Tom Smellie**, *Hockley Valley Brewing Co.*—Andrew, you are a fine brew master and I truly appreciate you sharing your brewing techniques and what makes you such a fine brewery. **Gottfried Boehringer**, *Stonemill Bakery*—thanks so much for sharing your wonderful facility with me, I hope to inspire everyone to eat fresh, healthy, tasty breads, like the ones you produce today. Thank you again. **Cynthia and Mike Beretta**, *Beretta Organic Farms*—Thanks for your contribution **Scott Lanau**, *Albion Orchards*—thanks for sharing your apple orchard with me, I hope to get more people coming out to wonderful places like yours. Keep up the great work! **Greg Downey**, *Berryview Farm*—thanks for sharing your asparagus farm and letting me in on how precious local farmers, such as you, are. **Anthony and Cheryl Dawson**, *Black Willow Elk Farm*—thanks for sharing your elk farm with me. You have a beautiful way with the animals and have brought me closer to how important it is to be in touch with where my food comes from. **Ralph and Julie Baumlisberger**, *Windy Field Farms*—you both opened my eyes to the beauty of a local mushroom farm. You both have a wonderful operation and am very pleased you took the time to share it with me so I may share it with others. **Bert Niewenhuis,** *Bert Niewenhuis (Lamb)* Bert—your farm is beautiful and I am so pleased that you took the time to share your farming facility with me. Your heart is in your farm and the animals and I am very happy ot share this experience with others. Thank you. **Gavin Dandy**, *Everdale Organic Farm*—thanks for showing me around your farm. It is people like you who are going to make the difference with our children today. You have definitely added some greatness to the book. **Bill and Wendy Masters**, *Knollbrook Farms*—you are both the most modest farmers I have met, with the utmost respect for your animals. Thanks for being so kind and sharing your farm with me so I can share it with others and inspire them to eat fresh and local. **Lou Maieron**, *Silver Creek Aquaculture*—Lou, you have an incredible fish farm, and thanks for sharing it with me. Not many people in our own community know you are there, so now I hope everyone gets to know where you are, and meet up with you and your wild Swan! You make a difference in the farming community. Thanks again. **Dan and Nina Garyfalakis**, *Hockley Valley Honey Farm*—thanks for spending as much time with my kids and I. It is obvious you love what you do. Now let's get everyone excited to support local organic honey! **Margaret and Paul Galati**, *Rock Garden Farm*—thank you. You both give the community a great place in the county to shop for the finest local produce. Thanks for sharing your market with me so I may share it with others. **Janine Livingston**, *Broadway Farms*—thanks for sharing your country market with me. It is people like you in a local community that bring us together and support each other. Keep up the great work! **Robert and Melissa Achal**, *Busy Bee Gardens*—dreams and visions are created by two young hard working people like the both of you. Thanks so much for sharing your lavender and your visions with me so I may share them with others. **Maggie and Johann Kleinsasser**, *Whole Circle Farms*—you are wonderful community people with organics in mind. You've chosen a more natural way to farm using bio-organics and I thank you both for sharing your way of farming with me. **Randy Leitche**, *Leitche's Honey*—thanks so much for sharing your passion for bees and your love of honey. You make it possible for people in the community to enjoy local honey. **Trevor Marshall**-Marshall Digitizing, thanks for your work on this project, long live solid relationships. **Hugh Sutherland**-*Carriage Trade Wines & Spirits* I would like to thank you dearly for your contributions, a toast to you!

Stacey's fabulous food journeys

Follow me on my fabulous food journeys, sharing with you how much fun you can have discovering what exisits in your own back-yard. Reconnecting with the way food should be. Journey through these pages and then move on to page 10 and 11 for more.

Winter

Spring

Summer

Autumn

Winter is the season when growing starts

Spring

Fresh, new sweet apple blossoms and buzzing bees

Summer is full of sweet fruits and tasty vegetables

Autumn

Excited about fresh fall squash and root vegetables!

A cookbook like no other

Within the pages of this unique cookbook you will find interesting features about a number of subjects near and dear to my heart.

LOCAL FOOD

We seem to be more obsessed with food than ever before. But did you ever take the time to ask *where is my food coming from?* I am taking you on a wonderful fun-filled food journey through my cookbook ***freshalicious™***. My visits to local farms, farmers' markets and producers will inspire you to get out and source local food in your community. I have lived the local lifestyle all my life but had a fantastic awakening when I was pushed to really see the benefits behind supporting local, buying local and eating within the seasons. So off we go! I leave no culinary stone unturned and hope to inspire you as I have been inspired by those in my community.

SOURCING FOOD CLOSE TO HOME

Sourcing food close to home is easier than you think. With farmers' markets opening everywhere, it seems this venue will be with us for a long time. We are greener and more conscious of our environment and concerned about our food. Farms feed cities, and knowing that I have locally produced food available to me gives me a great sense of comfort. As it should you too. We have at our finger tips, grocery stores that support local, farmers' markets, sideroad fruit and vegetable stands, and farmers all around us willing to give us the freshest, best-tasting foods right in our own backyard. Grocery store shopping will never be the same once you become enlightened to all the possibilities regarding your food. What I love most about sourcing local is that your carbon footprint is greatly reduced immediately. Can't beat that!

FRESH INGREDIENTS

Who wants to cook tonight? I certainly do. Cooking food from fresh is a simple and easy way to get the most from the food that you eat every day. It literally takes minutes to cook up fresh vegetables and season them with sea salt and sunflower oil. It takes no more than seven minutes to cook some chicken breasts with mushrooms. Why not take 10 minutes to cook local fish and sprouts? Your most nutritious and fulfilling meals actually come from eating fresh. I believe that you feel less hungry after eating home cooked meals and will have less food cravings throughout the day.

So when you're at the drive-thru, thinking you're saving time you're actually just cutting into your health and well being. The time saved now may cut years off your personal health, future quality of life and how long you may live. Bold but true. We take the time to buy the best clothes, the hottest new phones, and the sexiest cars, so why not try sourcing fresh ingredients? It will give you a great reason to cook tonight!

PROCESSED FOODS & FAST FOOD

Does it ever occur to you that going to a grocery store these days is like sending a kid into a candy store? The kids are you and I! The majority of what is inside is packaged neatly into boxes, plastic bags, containers and millions of cans. The food is hidden neatly inside with a beautiful picture on the front, which rarely looks like the real thing, and has limited good taste. What holds it together and keeps it fresh and how does it stay colourful? Fresh food does not have the ability to stay on the shelf for long before it rots. What can be an eye-opener for you is some of these foods will not rot for up to a year, nor will it lose its shape or colour. Ahhh, does that not make you think about what you're consuming, and what happens to it when it gets into your body? You can think about that one, because I do not want to know personally. I would rather avoid it! And what's up North America, are we all turning into mush? Have a good look at yourself if you're a fast foodie. Is your skin pale? Are you overweight?

What about lazy and tired all the time? Mostly I bet you have incredible food cravings. And what the heck, do you have a dirty car to boot? We are completely overwhelmed with the number of fast food outlets on every street corner. A burger for a buck! Where is the salad, the vegetables or the whole-grains? Living in a processed fast food world is just a bad habit we have all picked up over time. I agree it is allowing us to accomplish more during the day, but as I have said before, by going this way we are reducing our living years and possibly creating serious future heath issues. What do preservatives, food colours, modified foods, excess sugar, processed foods and excess amounts of fast foods do to your body inside? Could it be that we are slowly being preserved?

MANY REASONS TO EAT DAIRY-FREE

As a mother of a daughter who is anaphylactic to dairy, I went through a lifestyle change. I read labels; as they do change. I look up food ingredients I cannot understand and I avoid foods that I feel are unfit for her, and for us. So what does eating dairy -free mean to you and I? If you're seriously allergic to anything you avoid it to stay alive. If you're lactose intolerant you avoid it because it makes you sick.

If you have diseases of the heart, or are overweight you can greatly reduce your caloric-intake and live a healthier life. Having blood-related problems, or high cholesterol can be one of the best reasons to eat dairy-free.

And if you're thrifty about food costs, dairy is expensive these days. If you choose to eat dairy free for any reason, calcium-rich foods are available at the same grocery store. I have listed some foods for you further on in the book (page 15) that you can work into your diet. There are other calcium supplements that your can use—we have found a fruit based calcium for the girls. Making lifestyle changes to accommodate you can be challenging, and this is why I have put together the *freshalicious*™ cookbook, to help you see how easy eating dairy free can be. We are used to the flavour-enhancing foods and have lost touch with what food really tastes like without dairy. Enjoy the change and try every recipe at least once!

HEALTHY EATING LIFESTYLE

You may notice once you get into the book that all the information I provide is to make healthy eating easier. It is simple and fun if you ***fokas***, oops I mean focus, on all the right things. If you're procrastinating, dieting, overeating and then binging and nothing seems to be working, it is probably because your not **"*fokased*"** yet. Taking this personal food journey helped me understand the importance behind healthy eating, sourcing local and making the best food choices for me and my family. The effects of not eating healthy are being felt by all us because we are too busy to be focused on the really important things in life and the main one is "the food we eat."

WHAT'S IN A LABEL?

There are so many food/nutrition labels. Most often labels are telling us things we need to know and often warning us about all the good reasons it should remain on the shelf! Have you ever wondered why there are no labels on apples or pears or celery? Really why there is a nutrition label on gum, is that not just silly? We all know there is no nutritional value in gum.

It is tough enough that food ingredient listings are sometimes confusing; often listing things we cannot pronounce or find a definition for. So why are we eating it? There is a false sense of reality in the grocery stores that whatever they have to offer for us to buy is good for us. Not really.

You and I need to be smarter consumers and make clearer choices when buying food based on how natural it is. Five or more ingredients is your first indication that there may be too many things that are not good for you. Then add into the mix someone with a serious food allergy. Not just milk, but peanuts, shellfish, seeds and nuts, gluten and the list goes on. Try leaving behind the glucose, the fructose, and the sodium. What about the nitrates, the sulfites and the dyes? And really who needs preservatives? Try buying the foods that have a label of origin and no nutritional label and you will see what I mean. Try making really nutritional healthy choices simply by buying fresh.

EXPONENTIAL BENEFITS

The exponential benefit of a healthy lifestyle can only be determined and felt by you. Simply eating fresh, local, healthy foods is just the beginning. Old habits can be turned into new ones. There are health benefits to be had by everyone who chooses to be inspired by a healthy lifestyle. My goal is to get as many people across North America inspired to eat fresh local and in season within your community. The benefits are not just personal for you but will be felt by all of us. Creating employment for farms creates purpose and wealth within all communities.

Totally awesome, something fresh and new that's really cool!

Ok! Gotcha! You picked up the *freshalicious*™ cookbook and you're curious. This is not just an average cookbook with just really great recipes. I have taken a fun-filled food journey to help inspire you to do the same. Everything we need is in our own backyards, and sometimes we are so overwhelmed we tend to look beyond and not realize what we have. This is my dairy-free life and I want to share it with you. I have created more than 125 recipes to share with you how we eat fresh delicious and dairy-free every day. Within this book are short stories that will inspire you to see how easy it is to source local within your community, and eat within the seasons.

I have been cooking dairy free for 10 years. When I entertain for family and friends, they are amazed at how delicious lasagna and pizzas can taste without cheese, or how amazing cookies and cakes taste without the extra calories from dairy! These recipes are for everyone who is looking to eat simple, fast, convenient, healthy, great-tasting recipes made right at home. I explain how to substitute ingredients when baking cakes and cookies without milk, butter or eggs Keeping the taste is incredibly fantastic!

Do we know what is going on with the food we eat today? Are we really taking the time to source locally and support our own communities? Are we moving too quickly to sit still and enjoy fresh healthy meals with our kids, friends and family? Eating out today seems to be a daily event. With some really good planning, a little structure and the right recipes, cooking at home with family and friends can be and should be easier than ordering a pizza.

When you look at fresh food what do you think? We seem to be obsessed with fat - low fat, no fat, too much fat. And what about the calories, carbohydrates and proteins? If we are currently obsessed with food in this way is it possible that we are not reading the labels any more? Are we buying fresh, delicious natural foods in their raw state? Sometimes I wonder if we are too distracted to notice what we are eating, its country of origin and what it contains.

Imagine if you arrived into this world, a newborn and you were anaphylactic to milk protein? You would hope that your parents learn how to take care of you and keep you from harm's way. How would you, as a parent, deal with the lifestyle change ahead of you that revolves around a food that you have eaten every day? You change your life, your eating habits and source out other ways to satisfy your dietary needs. You stop eating out at restaurants and start cooking everything at home. The same lifestyle change takes place if you are diabetic, lactose intolerant, suffer from obesity or other health-related problems and you want to continue living as healthy as possible. Maybe you are looking to just find a healthier way to eat so you look for a lifestyle around food that suits your needs. My life changed to accommodate my eldest daughter's food allergies as she was born allergic to all milk ingredients, eggs, olives, olive oil, tomatoes, lemons and sulphites. She has outgrown all the food allergies, but she's still anaphylactic to milk. All the more reason to really care about food and the food we eat.

In talking with family, friends, and acquaintances about living a dairy-free lifestyle, the most common reaction is,"Well, what do you eat if you do not eat dairy?" Like it's the only available food source! I laugh, and say, "Well, everything you eat without the dairy!" and they laugh with me of course! Taking on the dairy-free lifestyle has brought positive changes to my family including my husband Steve. He started to lose weight and his cholesterol levels dropped. He has avoided being put on medication and eats more food than he ever has and is able to control his weight.

Choosing to eat fresh foods close to home and in season tastes better since the produce is typically fresher and picked closer to the time it is ready to be harvested. This means you would be consuming food that would require fewer preservatives, less packaging thereby greatly reducing your personal carbon footprint. We are so accustomed to having whatever we want, whenever we want when it comes to food. Maybe we have lost the true appreciation for the local farms that may not have a future if we don't start making a lifestyle change to keep them around for us to enjoy. When you have been afflicted by food allergies, it matters where your food comes from. You need to trust what you're buying, and know that it has been grown using safe farming practices, safe packaging, and proper safer labelling.

Everything you need is right in your own backyard. My "local" is from sea to sea, within my local community encompassing North America. Why not take my local concept and try it in your community? My dairy-free lifestyle can be utilized in Toronto, Canada, just as easily in Los Angeles, California or to the east in New York City. Sourcing local first is the key; sourcing on the same continent is absolutely necessary to protect our local food suppliers. Utilizing simple, fresh, delicious in-season recipes makes it all that much more fun and interesting. My intention is to inspire you to really think about your food in a new way, not just for convenience, or cost, but for how great food can actually taste. All done right at home and dairy-free, prepared by you in your kitchen.

I would love to hear from you! Visit my website and send me your comments. I specialize in taking your favourite recipe and tweaking it to be healthier, without sacrificing the taste, answering all your questions regarding local, in-season and dairy-free cooking. I can do all of this for you, just go to **www.freshalicious.ca.**

I am passionate about cooking really great tasting food that is simple, easy to prepare and healthy. Recipes like these are for everyone. Enjoy my recipes, cook with love and passion, slow down a little, and really enjoy life to the fullest!

What I discovered on my fantastic food journeys

What I found really interesting is you can learn about yourself by watching others, and if you do not take the time to get out and see how wonderful your community is through your local food, you don't know what you're missing! So be inspired! Get out and have some fun!

GROCERY STORE SPY

Look around next time you're out shopping. Become a grocery store spy—check out other people's shopping carts and get the big picture. We are not always our own best critic, but look at what others are buying. It seems easier to identify what someone else is doing wrong than what we may be doing ourselves. Who has a cart full of boxes, sugary sweets, white bread and frozen prepared foods? Who has a cart loaded with fresh local produce, whole grain-bread, fruits, local chicken and beef?

It is all about you and your body—making healthier choices makes a healthier you. So next time you're out and about, be more aware of what you may be filling your cart with.

FOODS I DISCOVERED CLOSE TO HOME

I am a country girl at heart. Ever since I was a small child I have taken a keen interest in what is produced locally.

I believe that we can all make a difference by focusing our shopping habits on fresh, locally produced foods that are unprepared, and cooking with our seasons in mind.

Ultimately, if you search for local suppliers as I have done, you will get the best, most nutritious foods available at prices comparable to those in the major grocery stores. If we create a demand for these foods, I am certain they will be more readily available to us. The larger grocery stores will support more locally once again.

Sharing our ideas with each other, discussing rumours, exchanging facts and talking about what matters are beneficial ways to monitor and cope with changes in our economic landscape. For our own future, health and welfare, we need to recognize how sensitive and precious our local food resources are.

I have traveled to local bakeries, farms, meat producers (including elk), fruit and vegetable growers, and some of the most beautiful wineries in our region. I was amazed to discover that almost everything we need is grown right in our own backyard. One notable exception is sugar, but maple syrup and honey are excellent substitutes.

Within 25 kilometres (16 miles), I found farm-fresh eggs, pastured (organic) beef, pork, fish, shiitake and blue oyster mushrooms, heritage tomatoes and potatoes, apples, cherries, asparagus, raspberries, blackberries, strawberries, corn, eggplant, cucumbers, peppers, pumpkins, squash of all varieties, pears, herbs, spelt oats, organic wheat, canola, chickens, geese, ducks, turkeys, fresh breads and a variety of baked goods and preserves, plus wines and micro breweries that produce great-tasting beer. A lot of fabulous fresh foods are available within a short distance.

An additional 25 kilometres (16 miles) from my home has us in a place called Holland Landing where they grow cauliflower, broccoli, shallots, celery and much more. My farthest journey—130 kilometres (81 miles)—took me to Cherry Avenue Farms in the Niagara area, where more than 10,000 fruit trees produce the finest cherries, peaches, apricots and yellow plums. You can pick your own fruit right off the trees or look for it in some of our local grocery stores.

In the same area, the vineyards of Château des Charmes offer excellent wines that are stunning in taste and quality.

There are countless numbers of fresh producers in the Niagara Region that we visit annually. They are all well worth visiting and supporting. For the most part, the Niagara Region supplies many local grocery stores in our area.

The variety of foods used in my cookbook were found at local markets, or on the farms where they were grown.We also have some community grocery stores that are supporting local, making my sourcing local much easier.It is up to you and I to adopt a strong belief that local is the best way to go.

WHY SUPPORT LOCAL?

Whenever we shop for price alone and buy goods that are not produced locally, despite their availability, something has to give. We affect our local economy, slowly eroding jobs in and around our own communities. Our automobile sector is a prime example of lost jobs, security and pensions and the same is happening within our food industry. Imported foods are causing job losses in Canada, affecting local farmers, producers and meat packers. This indirectly is affecting you and narrowing your food choices.

We need to keep our local food sources viable for the future. Keeping our hard-earned dollars within our country is the sensible thing to do, and creating awareness is just the beginning.

You and I can do our part to encourage big grocery stores to buy and support local producers by continuing to request more local foods be available at their locations. We are seeing a few major grocery stores offering and supporting local, but by far not enough. If you read the labels, you will still find that a lot of foods, even when in season here, are imported from outside Canada. Why is that?

Partially because we the consumers, have all been too busy to notice. For the most part, our food is being bought for price and not for value. And without concern for where it originates. Even when in-season local foods are available, they are up against less expensive imported foods. This definitely affects local farmers and sometimes and maybe more often than we think, leaves them at a loss. Eventually they may end up deciding to change careers and no longer choose to be there for us. Often this may happen, not by choice. Our demands to everything all season long helps create this kind of environment.

We can protect our communities, farmers and producers, simply by eating local, keeping an eye on seasonal foods, and choosing to cook using them when in season. Eating imported foods once in a while may help us see how fortunate we are, and that there is a soild reason to not take our food for granted. Love your local food and where it comes from.

HOW FAST DOES FOOD ACTUALLY NEED TO BE?

It's tough living in a country where fast food is everywhere and available at all hours of the day and night. It seems prepared and packaged foods are being consumed more than fresh foods. If you take a look at the average North American grocery store, you will see the majority of the store is full of prepared foods. They are there because of you and me.

What are we teaching our kids about nutritional value when they are not eating fresh at the dinner table? They're learning to *live fast and eat fast.* There are no health and nutritional benefits by choosing to live this kind of lifestyle. More and more studies today are demonstrating that there is a definate relationship between how processed and prepared foods and health issues. Taking time and simplicity into consideration, my priority is to make my kids healthy; feeding them nutritional foods that take me little time to prepare. I am sharing this with you, so you may live a heathier lifestyle too.

Making the preparation of food part of a routine always helps. Pre-cooking large amount of vegetables is one way to get the family to eat them, and having fruit readily available on the countertop works, too. Keeping it simple, fun and interesting is one of the best ways to implement healthy eating.

With some really good preparation, simple recipes and a plan, we can be the source of our own fast food.

MAKING EATING OUT, HEALTHY AND LOCAL

In my community we are rich with casual dining restaurants. Almost all of them source local and cook within the seasons. They all have amazing chefs, that love to create fine food, and carry some of the finest wines. Everyone I know loves this kind of dining experience, whether they are in the inner city, or dining at the Inn, off a country road. These unique dining expereinces are all about fresh, local and healthy. So get out and enjoy!

Valuable tips on cooking and baking without dairy

I have taken 10 years to research and formulate great recipes without dairy. I thought it was important to share some tips and tools to make dairy-free cooking real easy! Just taking the time to cook at home, preparing simple great tasting food is just the begining.

GOOD NEWS ABOUT CANADIAN MILK

An interesting piece of information I would like to share is that, in Canada, we have tight regulations in place for our milk production.

In Canada it is illegal to use artificial growth hormones to increase lactation in cows. Similar to Europe, BGH (Bovine Growth Hormone) is banned here. It is illegal to sell milk that contains antibiotics in Canada.

Consumers of milk should be concerned about these important issues and should applaud our government for these regulations. We have very important policies in place to protect some areas of the food industry.

COOKING WITHOUT DAIRY

My life changed to accommodate Anastasia's food allergies. It took seven and a half years for her to outgrow several food allergies except milk. I have met many people over the past 10 years who are looking for ways to cook without dairy for several reasons and or including allergies and sensitivities to milk and dairy products. So why not share my tips and recipes with you.

Anastasia's food allergies have prompted me to create simple, fresh, delicious recipes that can be used by everyone. It is all about layering flavours. What intrigued me is that people who are eating my cooking want to learn how to cook without dairy because they love the taste. I have personally found that cutting out the dairy helps shed the pounds.

In my opinion, cooking without dairy just tastes better. Plain and simple. If you love dairy and have no reason to cook without it, try a recipes and compare so you can taste the difference for yourself.

In some cases, as with mine, you may simply have no choice, which has given me the opportunity to help others who want to adopt a dairy-free lifestyle.

The same lifestyle change may be necessary if you are diabetic, lactose intolerant, suffer from obesity or other health-related problems and you want to continue living as healthy as possible.

Or maybe you are looking to simply source a healthier way to eat so you look for a lifestyle around food that suits your needs.

SUNFLOWER OIL

Sunflower oil is my oil of choice when baking and cooking. It works perfectly in all applications. Cookies and cakes are lighter, and taste really great. Sunflower oil seems to bring out the natural food flavours in vegetables and enhance the taste.

Sunflower oil makes everything taste great with no aftertaste, allowing the layers of flavour to come through. It just tastes great!

NON-HYDROGENATED PRODUCTS AND PURE LARD

When baking for certain textures, and in specific recipes, when you cannot substitute oil for butter, I use Fleischmann®'s non-hydrogenated margarine or pure non-hydrogenated lard. Simply, the more natural the better. Hydrogenated products, or foods containing them, are to be avoided whenever possible.

It is important to note that the ingredients list on the label must state "non-hydrogenated" and not just say so in the product name itself—or simply-say "pure lard". I am aware of only one non hydrogenated product that I use in my cookies and that is Tenderflake®. It helps me make the best tasting baked goods. My Salty Cardamom Cookie Dough recipe calls for it, so try it. I am certain you will love it!

APPLESAUCE IN BAKING AS AN EGG SUBSTITUTE

When someone is allergic to eggs, you can still accomplish a well-formed, moist and tasty cake or muffin by using ¼ cup of applesauce in place of 1 egg. It really works!

To make sure it rises properly, add one more teaspoon of baking powder to the recipe just to be on the safe side.

If you achieve a moist cake or muffin following these techniques, you have succeeded. I have been making my cakes and muffins this way for ten years, in many flavours. They get eaten quickly.

SOYA, ALMOND MILK, RICE MILK OR JUICE

I like to substitute juice for milk liquids whenever possible. For instance, if you're after a raspberry flavour use raspberry juice; it works well and adds to the full flavour of whatever you're baking.

Apple juice is the most discreet alternative as it tends to take on the flavour you are already working with, while typically not giving the baked item an apple flavour.

Soya milk and rice milk also work very well, but you will get a different texture in your baked goods when using them. Rice milk is light, soya is dense and heavy. Almond milk is perfectly creamy.

I have found that the shelf life of a baked muffin is shorter when using soya milk.

You need to experiment with these options yourself to see which one creates the result that you prefer. Tastes may be different, as well as textures!

FRESH FRUIT CREATES A MOIST CAKE OR MUFFIN

Instead of always using bananas, try baking with local in-season fruits and using an amount equal to the bananas in your recipes. For example, 1 cup of bananas = 1 cup of crushed raspberries.

Fresh fruit in cakes allows you to bake with added nutritional ingredients. Change it up a bit and be creative using in local in season fruit!

Baked goods are not meant to be just sugar and flour—we should try to avoid these. Fresh fruit adds moisture, texture and real flavour to whatever you're cooking. This will add to the overall nutritional value of all your baked goods.

BAKED PASTAS AND LASAGNA

Many of my friends suggested buying soya cheese as a cheese substitute when I was first faced with eliminating dairy from my cooking. Most people think that soya cheese has no milk. Caution: read the ingredients.

I found that most of them contain casein which is a *milk protein* used as a binding agent, and that is exactly what Anastasia is allergic to!

I make my main pasta and lasagna dishes with generous amounts of sauce and extra oil and water to fill the spaces.

Checking your dish as it cooks will help you determine if you need to add more water as you go. There is no exact measurement per recipe as this is done by eye and depends how your oven bakes.

Using fresh local vegetables in place of cheese is also a great way to make baked pastas. Try using fresh Swiss chard, zucchini, peppers, eggplant, arugula or spinach. Avoid using frozen veggies, as fresh veggies always taste much better!

Remember, baking your pasta dishes with no-dairy greatly reduces calories!

ALTERNATIVE SOURCES OF CALCIUM

If you are in our situation and need to avoid dairy, I have put together a simple list of calcium-rich foods. The label may give you a good indication of the actual serving size that you may need on a daily basis.

Soy beverage, almond/rice beverages (fortified), orange/grapefruit juices (calcium fortified), salmon with bones, sardines with bones, soy nuts, collards, dandelion, figs, broccoli, kale, almonds, brussel sprouts, tofu (firm), rhubarb, spinach, okra, white beans, baked beans, peas, and bok choy.

Calcium in liquid and pill form is available for those who feel they are not getting enough. We use a liquid fruit-based calcium to supplement our daily calcium intake. Most calcium-based supplements are milk-based, so read carefully when buying a calcium supplement.

For more information on appropriate quantities seek the advice of your physician, pharmacist or dietician. Eat well and you will have no worries!

Simple fun suggestions for the busy lives we live!

We all love to share the next best thing! Some of us have taken the time to discover our kitchens, others are so busy we have not had the time to get there yet. Keep in mind with a little planning, these are a few simple things that you may want to do to make your days a little easier.

PREPARING AND COOKING FRESH VEGGIES

If you're guilty, then so am I. Have you ever boiled your vegetables too long and haven't tried them any other way? Keeping things interesting and changing how we prepare vegetables is the key. Kids get bored, so do you. Variety is the spice of life, variety makes happy tummies too!

Some of the best prepared vegetables are blanched in hot water for a few minutes, or pan seared. Baking, sautéing and broiling veggies are definitely more interesting ways to bring out different flavours that are in the vegetables.

I like taking the time to cut the vegetables with care, utilizing the natural shapes within the vegetable to make your dish more visually pleasing. Maybe if we work with the natural shapes and don't try to trick our children by mashing or hiding them in something, they may enjoy them more. Try the Kids Veggie Wedges. Kids love them and it's a great way to use in-season fall veggies. Sometimes balsamic vinegar and freshly-squeezed lemons are a great way to season your veggies You can easily BBQ broccoli, cauliflower, zucchini, tomatoes, eggplant, okra it all tastes great. Simple 9-minute veggies that taste great!

As broccoli and cauliflower become available, I get out the garlic (fresh or powdered), sea salt and fresh lemons, a sheet of foil, and go to town! I cut them into tiny florets so the cooking time is reduced to a few minutes.

When I am really in the mood for intense flavour, I leave them on to get a brown and roasted appearance — the taste is amazing! There is nothing wrong with barbecuing zucchinis, tomatoes and eggplant drizzled in oil and seasoned with sea salt! Having fun, being creative can completely change the way you eat your veggies!

PIZZA ON THE Q!

What better way to cook pizzas than on a stone in the Q. We personally love to cook pizzas all summer long on the BBQ. That taste is unbeatable —crunchy bottom and a little smoky. The time is comparable to the oven but the taste exceeds what the oven produces. Investing in a pizza stone is definitely a great move for pizza lovers.

Think about making fresh homemade pizza dough. Try my pizza recipes and my unique way of cooking pizza and you will see how you can have a healthy, lower-cal way to enjoy the all-American favourite! Low cal and dairy-free.

MY FAVOURITE KITCHEN TOOL IS THE PRESSURE COOKER

What more can you ask for? This is an old traditional favourite pot that cooks your food often in only 10-15 minutes while locking in all the flavours. If you're pressed for time like I am, this was the best kitchen investment that I have made.

Pressure cookers are simple, easy to use and cut down preparation and cooking times. On a tight budget, try the tastier tougher cuts of meat and create a fabulous stew. They all come with instructions for use and the best model I have found is the one with the lid that bends into the pot with safety triggers that will only let you open the lid once it let the pressure out to a safe level. Soups can take 8-10 minutes; you can cook beans in no time. With busy, crazy lives today this is a cooking tool that no kitchen should be without!

A SECOND FRIDGE FOR FRUITS AND VEGGIES!

Do you get fed up with an over-crowded fridge where things spill, get tucked away, and start to reproduce something new? This is the easiest way to create a really neat science experiment! So why not invest in a second fridge that is energy efficient where you can create the space fresh foods need?

If there is not enough room in the kitchen, you can put it in the basement or in a secondary room. The second fridge works well for us, and we open the door less, keeping the contents fresh a little longer. It seems having a well organized fridge to go with the kitchen, along with proper storage space makes all the difference in how often we tend to prepare those fruits and veggies.

GREEN PAN CAN HELP CUT THE FAT!

I have been using the Green Pan® line for a while now and highly recommend the line to anyone who loves to cook. They are simply the best pans I have ever used. Its non-stick properties are absolutely wonderful and the fact that no toxins are released while cooking is fantastic!

I also discovered that you can use a lot less oil when cooking with the Green Pan.® I am an absolute oil fiend and do not get overly concerned about how much sunflower oil I use as long as it comes out tasting great. If you need reduce the amount of oil for whatever reason, this pan cooks really great with less oil at lower temperatures. The key is finding a pan that works for you. A friendly tip—if your pan tends to get sticky, reseason it with oil, turn up the heat for a few minutes, wipe clean and your good to go.

FOOD VISIBILITY - REARRANGE YOUR KITCHEN? WELL, WHY NOT?

Why not start a nice collection of glass jars with lids to store your dry goods in? It is really interesting when you open the kitchen cupboards to see the beans, or the whole-wheat pasta, dark brown rice. It is visually pleasing and may help you decide what your next *fresh delicious* inspiration will be. Having all the staples right in plain view can bring out the best in all of us when creating new dishes. Why not inspire yourself?

We buy food in all sorts of containers and boxes, and the cupboards get so cluttered that we often forget what is inside. We cannot see the food within and often become uninterested in it because we only see a box.

Let's not forget that boxes of food do expire, and may not stay as fresh as we would like. My friend Rose has taken this concept one step further and put glass doors on her cupboards so she can just see what is inside without opening the doors. Food is beautiful, why should we hide it? Glass jars are the best place to store foods in, easy to see keeping it and fresh. Kitchen reorganization is one of my specialties—a neat, organized and visually pleasing space is a very good space to work in which to work.

COOK WITH THE KIDS

I know it's really tough for all of us to go home after a long day, and start to cook for the family. Most often we ask the kids to go and play while we prepare dinner. In my house, when I was small my parents did not get home right away so we learned to cook and prepare foods at an early age to help out. I don't recommend that you put your kids to work in your absence, but allowing them to help and participate in the kitchen is a great learning experience. It gets them motivated to learn how to cook under your supervision, and learn about nutritional foods and start participating in choosing tomorrow's menu. Cleaning the dirt off the carrots, or cutting off the celery ends are all part of the fun! It establishes a connection with fresh food preperation. I feel it is important that kids know where their food is coming from and that they get involved in cooking as soon as they are able. By doing this, they build a strong bond between themselves and the healthy choices they will be making in their future. Before you know it they will become fine little chefs!

TRY COOKING EXCESS FOR THE NEXT DAY

Cooking excess food today makes your next day just that much easier. There will always be something healthy in the fridge for the kids when they come home from school. You are helping them make healthy food choices by being prepared in advance. Gives simplicity to day to day living.

Most foods, when prepeared fresh at home, taste better the next day. There is no longer a need for prepared packaged foods when your in charge.

The next time you're preparing dinner, cook more than just enough, making your life a whole lot easier and less costly. Those pre-prepared foods are expensive, often tough to digest and are definitely not **freshalicious™**!

We need to make time to live a healthier lifesytle. Thinking ahead and being prepared are the most important considerations. Once you start implementing a heathier lifstyle, you will see the real connection between all the things I talk about in this book. Simple and healthy living.

PROCESSED FOODS VERSUS FRESH UNPROCESSED FOODS

Processed foods seem to have become a large part of the North American diet. Quick, easy, low -nutritional foods packed with preservatives, sugars, starches and fillers. Take a quick look through your pantry, fridge and freezer. Do you have a lot of processed foods hanging around the house? Bet ya do!

Take the time to start replacing these bad habits with some good ones. Instead of burying them in the fridge, try displaying fresh fruits, like apples, pears, grapes and peaches on the counter within easy reach so they can help themselves.

Recent studies conclude that processed meats can be very unhealthy since they are typically high in sodium and that they contain things like corn syrup solids and nitrates. They are also very expensive. You can look for the real cooked meats that look real and are not processed, or you can always cook up a tray of chicken breasts for sandwiches, make good ole egg salad or tuna. My personal favourite is oven baked vegetables.

When choosing pre-packaged foods try looking for whole, healthy natural snacks and do not get too caught up in the low-fat fad. Good oils are good for you; try to pick foods that look like they do in their original or whole state. Foods like raisins, dried apricots, almonds, dried cranberries and whole- grain foods are all better food choices than many products we see on the shelf today. Cereal bars tend to have high amounts of corn syrup and lots of sugar, as do a lot of cookies and crackers which may stimulate food cravings. Look for natural healthy alternatives, high in fibre and low in fat and refined sugars. As natural as possible.

BOXES, PACKAGING AND POLLUTION

Did it ever occur to you that the need to have super convenient boxed foods actually pollutes our world in ways that you would never imagine? Why are we not talking about box pollution? The impact on the environment is greatly related to how we are buying our food, how we are not preparing it as often as we should. Just think about food in its natural state; if you buy it raw it either comes in its own skin with little or no packaging. It's usually delivered on a wooden skid, and if grown locally, very little fuel is used to transport it.

Anything that is pre prepared uses a lot of energy, trees, metals, dyes, chemicals, electricity, gas and fuel (transportation). Before it gets to your table it has burned up a tonne of resources.

Most of us are so busy today that the thought of this has probably not crossed our minds. Yes, we are all too busy and want convenience but at what cost? What is really scary is that kids are growing up today in such a fast food, fast-paced environment and do not know the repercussions of this kind of lifestyle. They see eating fast food as cool and interesting. Fancy, colorful and chemically-enhanced foods are seen as nutritious and fun! We are "the creators" of recycling and poor diets. When I grew up, we did not have blue boxes "nothing was recycled like it is today. It was typically re-used and put to use, not reuse and what do we do with it now..... Foods were often contained is sustainable packaging like glass, not plastic and cardboard. Recycling is a way to deal with a huge mess that is in existence solely for our convenience.

One challenging issue that I see in the recycling realm is that according to statistics, North America only recycle approximately 4% of the recyclable waste that we produce. That is it! It's estimated that every time you put out your Blue Box, 96% still goes to landfill! Of course, this varies from region to region." We have moved so far ahead and so fast with producing garbage, but don't have enough facilities, or dollars to deal with the problem.

The negative impact is being seen in our oceans today and directly relates to the food we eat every day. Studies show that there is enough plastic floating in the Pacific Ocean to cover the United States twice! Chemicals are leaching into our food chain, poisoning the food in our seas.

What about rivers and lakes, and the soil we grow

our fruits and vegetables in? We are, perhaps unknowingly, contributing to polluting the dirt, the water systems, the air we breathe utlimately our bodies, simply by the way we eat and buy our food.

However there is an immediate solution for such a huge problem. Buy local sustainable foods, support local in every way possible. Since we eat at least three times a day, 7 days a week, 365 days a year, how much garbage and recycling can we reduce by changing our eating habits?

I think this is one of the fastest ways to contribute to a cleaner, greener environment and lower our carbon footprint immediately. Next time you go to the grocery store, think about your personal impact and how you're making a huge difference immediately by buying fresh, unprepared foods that are locally produced and locally grown.

You will start by saving money on your grocery bill, recycling less and producing less garbage for the garbage man. Your impact on the environment will be greatly noticed right away. We will see change immediately in our own homes, on the land and in the oceans.

We cannot afford not to change, corporately and personally! We can all contribute to less boxes, plastics, chemicals, and an unnecessary use of gas, oil, and emissions today through a simple change of habit. Our contribution to being socially responsible is just the beginning.

Food allergies and labeling from a child's point of view

READING THE LABEL

Reading food labels is not always easy as all foods are labeled differently. In talking with friends, family and business associates, most people do not take the time to read the labels on food products. Since I started talking about reading labels, they quickly realized that they do not really know what is in the food they are eating, or where it is from. Well what about all the other things listed that are either hard to understand or are not good for us? It is important that whatever food product we buy, we have a full understanding of the ingredients listed.

Really good healthy, natural foods tend to have less than five natural ingredients. Typically extra ingredients are added to increase the shelf life of the product, hold the colour, and or hold the flavour. This can be avoided by buying fresh and local.

It has been easy for me to make a mistake and buy something for Anastasia that contains milk because of how it is labeled not just what the ingredients listing says. Allergy labeling should also be clear and close to the ingredients. All too often I have purchased something and the warnings were not to be found until I got home, or Anastasia found them. Sometimes they're tucked away, so if you're reading for allergy related reasons, whether it be for a friend or a relative, please be careful as it is easy to overlook as labels do vary quite a bit.

The best labels come in the form of a fresh product, fresh does not have an extended shelf-life.

LAFF

I asked Anastasia one day to write a letter for me talking about her food allergies and how she feels. As her mom I really know how she feels, but as she gets older she changes the way she feels. She has made it clear that she does not mind having the milk protein allergy as she feels quite healthy without it. She is, however, really concerned with food labeling and believes that foods are not clear enough with their allergy warnings. We have made several mistakes, even after 10 years of reading labels and would like to see some simplicity behind this type of labeling. We have noticed that milk is in a lot of foods today, as are trace warnings. She always says to me "Mommy, why can't they just manufacture things without milk?" Why does there need to be milk in bread? Why are there traces of milk on sunflower seeds? She loves sunflower seeds and rarely do we find them without traces of milk. And why not have chocolate without milk? Try to explain to a 10-year-old how the factories package different food items. She is missing out on truly nutritional foods all the time because of these warnings. One day she would love to see all food without traces of milk, and or labeled correctly so she can eat what she likes without having to put it back on the shelf. And if milk traces exist, that it be properly labeled, unfortunately this is not what is being done today.

"Mommy, why can't they just manufacture things without milk?"

Together we have created LAFF, Little Allergy Food Friends, to help educate children and adults live better with food allergies. Food allergies are becoming quite common in schools today. There also seems to be some anxiety among children and parents who do not fully understand serious food allergies. Oddly enough, even today, most people assume that Anastasia is lactose intolerant, when we say she is anaphylactic! The LAFF children's book is designed to offer the kids a positive way to help their friends cope with food allergies. We are so excited to launch this book for all the kids and parents who are living with food allergies!

NO SHELLFISH™
NO EGGS™
NO DAIRY™
NO SEEDS™
NO NUTS™
Sugars / Sucres 8 g
Vitamin C / Vitamine C
Calcium / Calcium
PIMENT DU CHILI MARIN
PAPRIKA.
OVEN BEFORE SPRAYING. DO NOT
ON HEATED BARBEQUE GRILL. DO
INTENTIONAL MISUSE BY
CANOLA OIL, SOY
TAINS: SOY.
monosodium glutam
turmeric, dehydrate
GLUTAMATE, DEHYD
AND ARTIFICIAL FLAV
CHICKEN FAT, YEAST
& DISODIUM 5'-GUAN
MONOSODIQUE, VIA
ARÔME NATUREL ET
SUCRE, GRAS DE
5'-INOSINATE DISODIQU

Winter is the season when growing starts

Winter in Canada! In many ways our winters can vary from year to year. Some winters can be mild and wet with lots of rain and others can be very cold with lots of beautiful snow!

Personally I choose the snow, as it is quite beautiful! We are so incredibly lucky to have four seasons in this country as our winters act as a natural pest controller, so as a country, we tend to use fewer chemicals during our growing season. This is better for us, better for the environment. Typically we seem to think our planting season is in spring, but our greenhouses are very busy planting seeds and getting a head start on a short growing season ahead. While the rest of us are still sitting by open fires or skiing down the slopes, tiny seedlings are quietly growing in warm sheltered greenhouses.

Before we know it we start to see fresh greenhouse tomatoes, cucumbers and peppers tempting us as we shop in the grocery store. The stage is set for the upcoming enjoyment of more fresh local produce.

Try to take a moment, as I do, when it seems like you have had enough of winter, and enjoy the important change of season. And take into consideration that growers are getting ready to produce the tastiest most healthy crops that will readily be available come early spring! The season is just beginning so let's get growing!.

december • apples • pears • carrots • asian vegetables • cucumbers • garlic • leeks • mushrooms • spanish onions • parsnips • cabbage turnips • onions • potatoes • squash • rutabaga • sprouts • squash • sweet potatoes • pumpkins • **january** • pears • apples • potatoes squash • beets • onions • cabbage • carrots • turnips • tomatoes • cucumbers • lettuce • peppers • garlic • leeks • mushrooms • parsnips • rhubarb • rutabaga • sprouts • sweet potatoes • **february** • apples • potatoes • squash • beets • onions • cabbage • carrots • turnips • tomatoes • cucumbers • lettuce • garlic • leeks • lettuce • mushrooms • parsnips • rhubarb • rutabaga • sprouts • sweet potatoes • peppers • **december** • apples • pears • carrots • asian vegetables • cucumb

WINTER

Get Growing!

Tasty perogie pizza

PREP

Serves a family of 4-6
Prep time: 10 minutes
Cooking time: Approx. 20 minutes

INGREDIENTS

pizza dough	1 large
potatoes yellow or white	6 large
spanish onion	1 large
sunflower oil	¼ cup
garlic powder	sprinkle
salt and pepper	to taste
fresh oregano	a few pinches

TOOLS

1 large pizza pan (vented)
1 large frying pan
1 plate for onions
1 large colander
1 large bowl for potatoes

TIPS

This pizza will only succeed if you prepare the potatoes by slicing them in cold water first and draining them in a colander before frying, otherwise they will stick together when frying them.

Preheat oven to 425°F.

Wash and peel potatoes and then slice them thinly in cold water.

Drain the slices in a colander so they are not wet when they hit the hot oil!

Slice and fry the onions in sunflower oil until slightly caramelized. Remove them from the oil and set them aside.

Cook the potatoes in the oil used for the onions, adding more oil if needed, until they become a little clear and start to brown.

Season them with salt and pepper and garlic powder, tasting as you cook them, so they are just right.

Roll out the pizza dough and place it on a vented pizza pan. Lay out the potatoes and onions on the dough, spreading them evenly.

When placing the potatoes on the pizza, make sure to use all the little brown bits. They absolutely taste the best!

Cook on the bottom rack until golden and you get that tantalizing aroma.

Place on a cooling rack, sprinkle with fresh oregano and cut while hot. Let cool and serve warm, the kids will love it!

PIZZA DOUGH SEE PAGE 206 FOR RECIPE

“A perfect pizza packed full of flavour. This is definitely one of my family's favourite pizzas.”

Creamy potato and leek chicken soup

PREP

Serves 4-6 (with extra for next day)
Prep time: 5 minutes
Cooking time: Approx. 8-10 minutes
(May take up to 30 minutes without pressure cooker)

INGREDIENTS

chicken legs with thighs	3 skinned
white onion	1 large
garlic cloves	2 chopped
sunflower oil	for frying
potatoes	8 large
sea salt	to taste
pepper	to taste
fresh dill	¼ cup
artisian baguette	1 or 2
leeks	2 sliced
wild rice	1 cup
water for rice	2 cups

TOOLS

pressure cooker (or large pot)
small pot or bowl for holding stock
1 small pot for rice
hand-held blender

TIPS

For moms and dads who are pressed for time and want really nutritious yet fast home cooked food, a pressure cooker takes care of both - reduced cooking times and the taste is unbelievable!

Wash chicken and boil in two cups of water for 15 minutes in uncovered pressure cooker or pot (until chicken turns white).

Cook wild rice in 2 cups of water for 20-25 minutes while preparing soup. Once cooked drain, season with seas salt and sunflowwer oil.

Remove from water and cool. Set water aside (stock) in a small pot or bowl.

Chop onions and garlic. Peel potatoes; cut large ones in half. In the pressure cooker or pot, fry onions in sunflower oil until clear, add garlic, fry for a few more minutes.

Add chicken stock from legs and up to 6 more cups of water, toss in potatoes, lock the lid, and boil for 8 minutes. (Up to 30 min. in regular pot, until potatoes are soft.)

Pull chicken from bones, break into pieces, set aside. Turn off heat, let out steam, and blend the soup adding sea salt to taste. Stir in chicken pieces and fresh dill.

Bring to a boil and simmer for a few minutes for the chicken to warm and dill to infuse into the soup.

Cooked this way, the chicken will be very tender and the soup exceptionally tasty!

Top each bowl with fresh ground pepper. Serve with a fresh baguette and a bottle of chilled white wine!.

“I love creating creamy soups less the added calories. They are perfect on cold winter days by the fire.”

Organic salmon steak with toasted flax seeds and wild blueberry sauce

PREP

Serves a family of 4-6
Prep time: 15-20 minutes
Cooking times: Approx. 3-4 minutes per side for the salmon, 10-15 minutes for the potato wedges,

INGREDIENTS

fresh salmon (preferably wild)	4-6 3oz pieces
sunflower oil	for frying
potatoes	4 medium
fresh broccoli	2-3 large
fresh cauliflower	1-2 heads
flax seeds	1 cup
fresh eggs	1-2
sea salt	to taste

BLUEBERRY SAUCE

wild blueberries fresh or frozen	1 cup
lemon juice	1 tsp
cane sugar or maple syrup	¼ cup
blueberry brandy	splash
cornstarch	2 tbsp

TOOLS

2 non-stick frying pans
1 large pot for blanching

TIPS

For the potato wedges if you want to speed up the cooking time, blanch in water for 10 minutes or until tender. Then fry them in the pan. You may want to remove skins-your preference. Always cook everything else before you cook your fish. Salmon takes very little time to cook and keeps cooking after it is served.

VEGETABLE PREP
Wash and cut the potatoes into ½ inch wedges, large enough to hold a salmon steak. Leave skins on.

Fry the potato wedges in sunflower oil until they are brown and thoroughly cooked. Cover to keep warm and set aside until the salmon steaks are cooked.

SALMON STEAK PREP
Toast the flax seeds in a very hot frying pan until they start to jump and pop! Put them aside on a plate to use on the salmon.

Steam or blanch the broccoli & cauliflower florets just before cooking the salmon, so they are ready to serve.

Beat the egg to create a wash to coat the outer edges of the salmon steaks. Sprinkle salt on the steaks, and dip the egg washed edges into the toasted flax seeds.

Fry the steaks on medium to high heat for 3-4 minutes per side.

Serve your salmon steaks on the potato wedges, lay the vegetables around the fish, and drizzle with the wild blueberry sauce.

BLUEBERRY PREP
Cook the blueberries for about 7 minutes with lemon juice, cane sugar or maple syrup,blueberry brandy (optional) and a drizzle of water.

Thicken with cornstarch. If it gets too stiff or thick, add water or juice to thin it slightly.

Château des Charmes Merlot,
St. David's Bench Vineyard, VQA St. David's Bench

Merlot Syrah-
Valdivieso Reserve Central Valley Chile or Casa Tamaya Reserve, Limari Valley Chile Hoo Roo Creek –Victoria, Australia, Cannonau di Sardigna-Tharru

“This healthy dish is packed with Omega 3, loaded with different textures to tickle your sensations... and to top it off plated to impress your guests!”

Fasolia (roasted lima beans)

PREP

Serves a family of 4-6
First prep time: overnight/ Next prep 10-15 minutes
Cooking time: Approx. 3-4 hours

INGREDIENTS

large dry lima beans	4 cups dry
carrots	4 chopped
celery stalks	4 chopped
chicken stock	2 cups liquid
tomato paste	½ can
scallions	4 chopped
sunflower oil	1 cup
dill	½ bunch
sea salt	to taste
fresh ground pepper	to taste

TOOLS

large bowl for soaking
11x15 glass pan

TIPS

This dish must be cooked at a high temperature and for a long time. Large lima beans, depending on how fresh they are and where they are from, may vary in cooking times. You will definitely need the afternoon to cook them, but it is well worth the wait as they taste fantastic for days afterwards.

Preheat oven to 425°F.

Soak beans overnight in 8 cups cold water and sea salt. You may need to add more water as they expand.

Rinse the soaked lima beans and put them into the large glass roasting pan.

Coat the beans with the seasonings and sunflower oil. Do not skimp on the oil, as it is the key to having them cook just right.

Mix in tomato paste, carrots, celery, scallions and chicken stock or a sprinkle of soup base. Stir in the tomato paste and cover completely with water.

Add half of the dill now and save the remainder to add ½ hour before cooking is done. Dill makes this recipe taste fabulous!

Cover with foil. Roast for 3-4 hours, checking often, adding hot water as necessary. These beans soak up alot of water while roasting at a high temperature, so keep an eye on them.

Add at least 2-3 cups of water throughout the baking time so they do not dry out.

Beans must be soft and cooked thoroughly.

“This is one of my favourites, exceptionally high in protein, and delivers great taste. If you are a Vegan or just love meatless dishes, this one is for you!”

Candied beef tenderloin with bean sprouts

PREP

Serves a family of 4-6
Prep time: 5 minutes
Cooking time: Approx. 10 minutes

INGREDIENTS

beef tenderloin	6-9 oz
orange liqueur	splash
bean sprouts	4-6 cups
sunflower oil	for frying
sea salt	to taste
baby bok choy	2-3
pomegranate seeds	handful

TOOLS

2 frying pans
1 pot

TIPS

To get your meat really thin, try slicing it when it is partially frozen using a professional knife; this is a really great investment!

Start by slicing the tenderloin into fine strips. Season and then fry them on high heat in a little sunflower oil and then add in the liqueur only and reduce for a few minutes.

Separate and wash the bok choy and blanch in salted boiling water for 2-3 minutes.

In a separate pan, with a little oil fry the bean sprouts on high heat for a few minutes and add sea salt to taste.

Cooking the sprouts too long will make them lose water and become mushy. They will continue cooking once you remove them from the heat.

Plate the bok choy first, then the bean sprouts, and top it off with the candied beef. Sprinkle with fresh pomegranate seeds and serve.

"Sometimes you just feel like having something really light, simple and incredibly low cal. Fresh local ingredients are easy to source."

Simple oven roasted red peppers

PREP

Makes enough for a few appetizers and baguettes
Prep time: 10 minutes
Cooking time: Approx. 1 hour

INGREDIENTS

yellow, red and orange	8 large
bell peppers	cut into ¼'s
garlic powder	sprinkle
sea salt	for seasoning
garlic powder	to taste
fresh garlic	4 cloves
sunflower oil	¼-½ cup

TOOLS

11 x 15 glass baking pan
foil

TIPS

The longer you cook peppers in oil and garlic and start to brown them, the more they taste like they came off the BBQ! Always keep the oil you cooked them in because it's infused with pepper flavour, it's really tasty, and can be drizzled over meats and rice.

Preheat oven to 400°F.

Wash the peppers and remove the top stems. Cut them into 4 pieces and remove the white flesh and seeds.

Lay foil on the bottom of the glass pan—no dirty dish with this one!

Place the pieces on the foil side by side. Drizzle with lots of sunflower oil and add the whole garlic. Sprinkle generously with garlic powder and sea salt.

Cover with foil and bake in the oven for 1 hour.

These can be undercooked or browned; the choice is yours. Try both ways! There is a big difference in the taste, depending on how long you cook them.

This is a quick and painless way to prepare really great tasting peppers in the winter for sandwiches, pizzas, snacks and small sides!

"I wanted to share with you how simple it is to capture the full flavour of roasting the peppers without all the muss and fuss of the BBQ."

Tiny whole wheat potato perogies

PREP

Serves a family of 4-6
Prep time: 20-30 minutes
Cooking time: Approx. 6-8 minutes

INGREDIENTS

DOUGH

whole wheat flour	2½ cups
plain soya milk	½-¾ cups
sea salt	½ tsp
sunflower oil	2 tbsp

PEROGIE FILLING

mashed potatoes	4-5 medium
cooking onions	2 medium
sunflower oil	¼ cup
herbs dill and/or basil	chopped
sea salt	to taste

TOOLS

1 large pot for boiling perogies
1 bowl to rest the perogie dough
1 large serving bowl for cooked perogies
1 frying pan
1 pizza cutter
2-4 non stick baking trays
2-4 tea towels to cover trays

TIPS

Perogies are a traditional Ukrainian dish usually made with potatoes and pressed cottage cheese, but they can also be made in many different flavours. My grandmother used to make really nice perogies with fresh apricots for the filling, or sauerkraut and onions. I like to flavour my potatoes with fresh herbs—dill, basil or thyme. Caramelized nuts work well in the filling, giving the perogie a whole new taste and texture experience. Feel free to experiment and try new things but, ultimately, the fried onions make the perogies complete!

MAKING THE DOUGH

Measure the flour and sea salt onto the countertop or in a bowl.

Make a well and gradually pour in the soya milk and oil. Knead until mixed; do not over-knead.

Roll into a ball and let it rest in the lightly oiled bowl for 30 minutes.

MAKING THE FILLING

Wash, peel and cut up the potatoes into small pieces to reduce boiling time. Boil in salted water until soft.

Cut the onions into very small pieces. Fry in sunflower oil until starting to brown. This is very important to get the right flavour. Remove from heat and set aside.

When the potatoes are soft, drain all of the water into a cup and set aside. Mash the potatoes—add some water and sunflower oil. Mix until smooth.

Mix in half of the fried onions, herbs, and sea salt to taste.

Put the other half of the fried onions into the large serving bowl and set aside. Let the potatoes and onions cool while the dough is still resting.

MULTIPLE FLAVOUR OPTION

Divide the potato filling into 3 bowls: 1 plain, 1 with fresh dill, 1 with fresh basil. If this is your first time, plain potatoes with onions are the way to go.

CONTINUES ON PAGE 40

“Using whole wheat flour and no dairy makes these perogies just that little bit more appealing for those who love great tasting, simply delicious comfort foods.”

Tiny whole wheat potato perogies cont'd

PREP

MAKING THE PEROGIES CONT'D

Roll out the dough nice and thin on a floured surface.

Set your trays close for the freshly made perogies. Have tea towels close by to cover the perogies so they do not dry out while making them.

Cut the dough into small squares, cutting in one direction and then counter slicing it the other way, approximately 2 inches per perogie.

I like to use a pizza slicer as it is quick, easy and makes nice straight lines. The squares will be folded corner to corner to become triangular perogies.

If you like semi-circular perogies, just use a small water glass with the edge floured to cut them individually. This leaves pieces that must be gathered together and rolled out again to cut more circles.

Place a teaspoon of potato filling on each piece of dough, one at a time. Using your fingers dab the dough edges with water, fold in half and pinch shut.

Lay the perogies on a tray and cover with a tea towel until you are done.

If you intend to freeze some, which you will, put the first tray(s) into the freezer right away uncovered. They may take at least an hour to freeze. Once they are, take them out and bang the tray to loosen them and put them in air tight freezer container.

COOKING THE PEROGIES

Boil a large pot of salted water.

Drop in 5-10 perogies at a time, whatever you feel comfortable with in that pot.

Cook until they rise to the surface. This will take 2 to 3 minutes when freshly made. Stir gently—do not let them sit on the bottom or they will stick!

Use a large spoon with draining holes to lift the perogies out when cooked.

Put them into the large serving bowl with the fried onions and lightly drizzle with sunflower oil.

Do not let perogies sit on one another without oil or they will stick! When cooking from frozen they will take about 8 minutes until done.

You can garnish them with chopped peppers, scallions or pan-fried garlic when serving them.

A perfect side dish for chicken cutlets and fresh garden salad.

“It is a good idea to double up on the recipe, they will keep in the freezer for those nights when your time is pressed for cooking.”

Sweet baked carrot and spicy pepper baguette

PREP

Serves 4
Prep time: 10 minutes
Cooking time: Approx. 30 minutes

INGREDIENTS

carrots	2 large
red bell peppers	2 sliced
oyster mushrooms	2-4 sliced
garlic cloves	2 chopped
dry hot chilies	sprinkle
sea salt	to taste
brown sugar	sprinkle
fresh thyme	2 sprigs
sunflower oil	drizzle
fresh baguette	1 fresh
arugula	2 cups

BALSAMIC DRIZZLE

balsamic vinegar	¼ cup
sunflower oil	½ cup
garlic powder	½ tsp
sea salt	to taste

TOOLS

2 glass baking pans
1 frying pan

TIPS

When roasting root vegetables it is always a good idea to start with a liquid. When they are almost done, set them under the broiler so they brown up nicely.

Preheat to 425°F.

Clean and peel the carrots; slice them, along with the peppers and mushrooms, so they are flat and can be easily eaten on a baguette.

Drizzle sunflower oil in one pan, add the peppers, and season with chopped garlic, chilies and sea salt.

In the other pan, place the carrots and sprinkle with brown sugar and season well with thyme and sea salt, then drizzle with sunflower oil.

Bake both pans uncovered for 15-20 minutes, until they brown and get crispy. Remove from oven and set aside.

Coat the arugula with the drizzle, you will want some left over for dipping, so use only what you need.

Fry the mushrooms in sunflower oil on high until brown; set aside. Slice the baguette into 4 sandwich style pieces and toast them under the broiler.

Lay on your arugula first, then the baked carrots, and then the spicy peppers. Add a drizzle of balsamic and top it off with the oyster mushrooms. Serve and enjoy!

Fantastically fresh, local ingredients made simple!

Château des Charmes Viognier,
St. David's Bench Vineyard,
VQA St. David's Bench

Viognier Gewurztraminer
Andert Gewurz- Austria, Calamus-Niagara-
Wunsch Mann Alsace France

“Being inspired by the season can bring out the best tasting simple sandwiches. Get inspired to create your own.”

www.freshalicious.ca

Pistachio and white wine roasted turkey legs

PREP

Serves a family of 4-6
Prep time: 5 minutes
Cooking time: Approx. 1½ hours

INGREDIENTS

turkey legs	4 skin on
soya sauce	for marinate
pistachios	3-4 handfuls
white wine	½ bottle
garlic cloves	4 whole
sea salt and ground pepper	to taste
sunflower oil	drizzle

TOOLS

1 large oven-friendly fry pan with lid or a cast iron pan

TIPS

When roasting turkey legs you can use other fruits such as apricots or plums along with a splash of brandy.

Preheat oven to 425°F.

Wash the turkey legs and place them in the pan. Bath them with soya sauce, drizzle with sunflower oil, sprinkle on ground pepper and crushed pistachios, and add a dash of sea salt for that extra mmmm!

Pour your white wine into the pan, toss in the garlic cloves, and into the oven it goes.

Roast uncovered for 15 minutes, then reduce heat to 375°F, cover and bake on the middle rack for at least an hour, until done.

How simple is that? Fabulous if served with tiny roasted potatoes and a salad.

This dish is unbelievably simple, and has an amazing taste.

“Fresh local turkey that is reared organically has great flavour. Coating the legs with crushed pistachios takes the turkey to a new level of taste!”

Turkey and sirloin lasagna with sweet carrots

PREP

Serves a family of 4-6
Prep time: 20-30 minutes
Cooking time: Approx. 40 minutes

INGREDIENTS

whole wheat lasagne	1 box
ground turkey	½ to 1lb
ground sirloin	½ to 1lb
spanish onions	2 medium
carrots	6 grated
diced tomatoes	1 can
crushed tomatoes	1 can
tomatoes fresh	3 grated
sunflower oil	¼ cup
brown sugar	½ cup
garlic cloves	4 chopped
oregano dried	1-2 tsp
thyme fresh	2-3 sprigs
sea salt	to taste
fresh ground pepper	to taste
corn flake crumbs	1½ cups

TOOLS

11 x 15 glass pan
1 frying pan
foil for lasagna
1 pot for sauce
1 large pot for lasagana

TIPS

When cooking lasagna noodles, try to undercook them and compensate with extra sauce and water, this will produce perfectly cooked noodles. As well, a little extra oil will make your lasagna turn out just right.

Preheat oven to 400°F

Start by simmering 1 can of diced tomatoes and 1 can of crushed tomatoes, season with sea salt, pepper, and a dash of brown sugar, while preparing the ground meat and lasagna noodles. Start to boil salted water.

Grate the carrots, season with sea salt and brown sugar, fry in the frying pan for 5 minutes and remove form heat and set aside.

Drizzle the sunflower oil in the pan with sunflower oil.

Chop and fry onions to caramelize them, and add the chopped garlic. Then fry ground meat with the spices and cook until all the meat is brown.

Grate 3 fresh tomatoes directly into the ground meat. Simmer for about 10 minutes.

Cook the lasagne noodles in a large pot of boiling, salted water for 8--10 minutes. Just a few at a time to avoid sticking. Dunk the noodles in cool water to stop the cooking, remove and drizzle with sunflower oil.

Start with the sauce, lay down the noodles, alternating meat, carrots and sauce.

Cover with foil and bake in the oven on the bottom rack for about 40 minutes.

“Sometimes just experimenting with new ingredients and a little sweetness can turn a brand new taste into an everyday favourite!”

Making old brewing traditions come alive at a local brewery

I was pleasantly surprised for many years at how many micro breweries exist in our local area. I am certain you can source one in your community too.

I was also shocked to discover that in Canada our largest breweries are no longer Canadian owned. It seems as the world changes so are the owners and original producers of food and alcohol-related products. Is this change good for the long term?

We all have a feeling that when any product is massed produced, something becomes lost. When it comes to really great tasting beer, there is a valued technique that a qualified brew master retains when crafting his product. This is all the more reason to source local and get in touch with local breweries. While I was out sourcing the locations of breweries I was so surprised to know that not even 10 minutes away from my home is a very well known brewery that I had the opportunity to have a good look at.

This is Hockley Valley Brewing Company. After meeting with Andrew, a master brewer with a long list of credentials in his field, I now have a better understanding about what makes a great tasting beer. He has spent quite a few years studying and training in Europe; knowledge he has brought back to Canada to brew award-winning beers.

Hockley Valley Brewing started in a 600-square-foot building. In December of 2002 a great Canadian brewing company was born. Little did they know their beer was going to be so well received. In 2005, 2006, 2007 and 2008, they received 10 Ontario brewing awards for their great tasting product — 9 golds and 1 silver!

Since we are so global and not local, we have too many choices it seems when we are out shopping for beer and spirits. I think in a way we are all spoiled and have lost sight of what we have around us.

Source out a local brewery in your neighbourhood.

Small micro breweries like Hockley Valley Brewing Company are going to make their beer week after week, offering the utmost quality because they want to keep you coming back to buy more. They are not interested in cutting corners for profit, but looking to keep their fabulous reputation.

Andrew and owner Tom work so well together in producing one great tasting beer. I must say that Andrew has a ton of expertise and a true understanding of how all traditional beers have been brewed for hundreds of years in Europe. They are all unique; based on ingredients; layers of flavours and brewing techniques. He is a true brew master and I thank him for sharing his facility. I hope this inspires you to source out a local brewery in your neighbourhood.

Local Beer
layered with natural flavours

Beer oregano roasted chickens

PREP

Serves 6-8
Prep time: 10 minutes
Cooking time: Approx. 1 ½hours

INGREDIENTS

local organic chickens	2 washed
large potatoes (skins on)	3 whole
celery stalks	3-4 whole
fresh carrots with tops on	1 bunch
fresh oregano	to taste
sea salt	to taste
fresh ground pepper	to taste
paprika sprinkle	for colour
sunflower oil	drizzle
local beer	2 cans
water	2 cups

TOOLS

1 large roasting pan
(large enough for two small chickens and vegetables)

TIPS

When roasting chickens you can change up the base flavour by substituting the beer for fruit juices like apple or pear juice. Try keeping the bones for soups the next day or create a stock that you can refrigerate or freeze for future use.

Preheat to 375˚F.

This is really my man's dish. No peeling, no chopping just rinse and toss into the roasting pan. It's all good. And how can you resist a chicken dish infused with beer?

How easy is this? Wash the birds in cool water, rinse the potatoes, celery, carrots and the tops, drizzle with sunflower oil, then season, add water and beer and you're done.

Cover with foil and toss in the oven at 375°F, roast until perfection. Typically, the chickens will be done around the same time the veggies are.

The size of your chickens will determine the time cooked. One way to check is to stick the chicken with a knife, it should pull back out easily and the juices should be clear.

“Simply delicious easy recipes that definitely make eating healthier and less challenging!”

Oven baked vegetables

PREP

Serves a family of 4-6
Prep time: 10 minutes
Cooking time: Approx. 45 minutes

INGREDIENTS

zucchini	5 small
eggplants	4 small
carrots	3 large
large green beans	3 handfuls
fresh tomatoes	2 grated
tomato paste	2 tbsps
garlic cloves	2 chopped
sea salt and pepper	to taste
sunflower oil	½ to 1 cup
brown sugar	¼ cup
fresh parsley	½ bunch

TOOLS

11 x 15 glass or ceramic baking dish
foil

TIPS

You can bake different vegetables together or just one kind at a time. Either way you will have a fantastic tasting dish made from fresh local produce! Pressed for time? The oven does it all for you!

Preheat oven to 400°F.

Wash all your vegetables.

Peel the carrots, cut them in half, and pinch the bean tops off.

Remove the ends of zucchini and eggplants (or leave as shown) and cut into chunks. Put all of the vegetables into the baking dish.

Dice, and toss in the tomatoes.

Water the tomato paste down and add to the mixture.

Add the garlic and spices, and pour the sunflower oil over the vegetables. Sprinkle the brown sugar and parsley on top and cover with foil.

Bake on the middle rack for at least 45 minutes, checking to see when the vegetables are cooked.

Ovens vary in temperatures, so adjust your time accordingly.

Image shown for 2 people

"Why boil when you can bake? With very little effort you can create amazing dishes with minimal cleanup."

Baked spelt fusilli with duck sausages

PREP

Serves a family of 4-6
Prep time: 10-15 minutes
Cooking time: Approx. 30-40 minutes

INGREDIENTS

local duck sausages	4 cut into pieces
sunflower oil	up to ¼ cup
organic spelt fusilli	250 grams
oyster mushrooms	5 sliced
fresh tomatoes	6 medium
tomato paste	½ can
water	2 cups
brown sugar	½ cup
fresh thyme	a few sprigs
dried bay leaves	2 whole
sea salt and pepper	to taste

TOOLS

11 x 15 glass baking pan
1 frying pan
foil

TIPS

When cooking a dish like this, remember that pasta takes up to 10 minutes to cook on the stove top, but at least 25 minutes or more in the oven. So we need to partially cook the sausages before hand. This also brings out the sausages' full flavour.

Château des Charmes Estate Bottled Chardonnay Musqué, VQA Niagara-on-the-Lake

Chardonnay Musque
Oregon Pinot Noir/Burgundy
Rafael Dubois Cote de Nuits, Chateau Saint Michelle

Preheat oven to 375°F.

Cut up your fresh duck sausages into chunks, removing the skin if you prefer. Sauté them gently in sunflower oil for 10 minutes, or until they start to brown.

Remove the sausages from the frying pan and set them aside.

Toss in the oyster mushrooms; fry on high heat to brown and bring out the flavour.
Set them aside.

Grate 3 fresh tomatoes into the glass pan. Then cut up 3 more fresh tomatoes and toss them in.

Put the sausages and fusilli pasta (uncooked) into the pan. Add your spices, brown sugar and bay leaves, covering all the ingredients.

Add water to fill the tray to the top and drizzle a little sunflower oil over the pasta.

Cover with foil and bake for up to ½ hour, or until the pasta is cooked.

Make sure you peek in on it and add hot water or more sauce if it starts to look dry.

“ Try using local lean duck sausages in place of pork and beef. This is one an easy way to introduce new foods to the family. ”
www.freshalicious.ca

Simple oven roasted turkey breast in white wine

PREP

Serves a family of 4-6
Prep time: 5 minutes
Cooking time: Approx. 1½ hours

INGREDIENTS

turkey breast organic	1 large
white onions	4-6 small
garlic	4 cloves
canadian white wine	½ bottle
sunflower oil	drizzle
ground sage	to season
sea salt and ground pepper	to season
sunflower oil	for drizzle

TOOLS

1 large ceramic baking dish with lid

TIPS

Turkey is one of those meats that take their own sweet time cooking, and it will remain moist if baked in a covered dish. Try sourcing local turkey, the taste and the texture is fantastic!

Château des Charmes Estate Sur Lie Chardonnay,
VQA Niagara-on-the-Lake

Chardonnay Pinot Gris/ Pinot Grigio
Klingenfus Winery Alsace France
or Colli Vicentini, Michel di Lisca Veneto Italy

Preheat oven to 400˚F.

Lay the turkey breast in the baking dish. Season it with sage, ground pepper and sea salt. Drizzle with sunflower oil.

Add the onions, garlic (skins on if you like) and wine to the dish.

Bake it with the lid on for at least 1½ hours, or until the breast is cooked and tender.

A knife should go in and out of the meat easily when it is done.

This is beautiful served with a blend of white and wild brown rice, and fresh asparagus.

"Let's talk turkey. It really is a great tasting meat, lean and full of flavour. Try roasting smaller portions, and source your turkey locally."

Stuffed sea shells with pork, chicken and spinach

PREP

Serves a family of 4-6 with extra for the next day
Prep time: 15-20 minutes
Cooking time: Approx. 1 hour

INGREDIENTS

large pasta shells	1 box
plum tomatoes	2 cups whole
fresh tomatoes	4 large
lean ground pork	1¾ lb
ground chicken	1¾ lb
sea salt and pepper	to taste
sunflower oil	¼ cup
cooking onion	1 large
fresh garlic	2 cloves
fresh spinach	1 cup
fresh dill	½ cup

TOOLS

11 x 15 ceramic or glass dish
1 pot for boiling pasta shells
1 bowl
1 frying pan

TIPS

Always prepare a dish like this right before meal time so it is still warm when served to guests. Try cooking some extra sauce for dishes like this to pour over when serving.

Preheat oven to 375°F

Boil the pasta shells in salted water 5-8 minutes to soften for stuffing. Rinse in cool water before handling.

Gently crumble the ground meat into a bowl. Add the sea salt and pepper and drizzle with sunflower oil.

Fry the chopped onion and garlic until they turn a little brown. Stir them into the meat mixture with a spoon, adding spinach, dill and all of the seasonings.

Squeeze the 4 tomatoes by hand directly into the baking dish and add seasoning. This gives you a chunky sauce as opposed to it being fine.

Add 2 cups of sauce to the meat mixture and start to stuff the shells. Lay your stuffed shells directly into the tomato sauce, side by side. Drizzle with sunflower oil and season with sea salt and pepper.

Add enough cold water directly into the dish to cover the shells, about 1-2 cups depending on your dish size.

Bake for 1 hour or so and check often, adding additional water if it gets absorbed. The pasta should be fully cooked, but not dry, and the aroma of this dish should make you very hungry!

Serving for 2 shown in image.

“Tiny stuffed pasta is a very traditional dish that the kids love. Simply perfect for next day lunches, and snacks.”

Keeping the art of making fine proscuitto alive

What do you think of when you hear prosciutto - Italy? Not local? One of the finest prosciutto suppliers is located in southern Ontario. You probably have one too, only you may have not found them yet.

I had the pleasure of meeting with Mario Pingue of Niagara Food Specialties, a family business that specializes in private label manufacturing of traditional Italian meats. What makes them even more interesting is that they use certified humane pork that is raised locally.

Not only does he produce the finest Italian prosciutto, but he has gained expertise and stands behind his processing techniques. In order to make a fine, unbelievable tasting prosciutto, you need to give it time to age and the initial preparation of the meat is vitally important. It requires a really good massage with sea salt and should be hung to cure. Important to Mario is buying locally raised, free-range or certified co-op meat.

> The utmost care is taken by the Pingue family to offer consumers nothing but the best

There are a few things to consider when buying cured meats. The most important thing would be to find a supplier like Pingue who uses natural processes in the production of his meats. In the more commercially produced environments you may find things like nitrates in the meat. This means that the producer has reduced time and sped up the process by using these preservatives. Nitrates are in a lot of processed meats, but we shouldn't be eating nitrates at all. They are not easily accepted by the body and too much of anything that is unnatural is definitely not something you want to be eating all the time. Pingue is all-natural and uses natural processes to produce very fine products. His secret is sea salt and time. That's it—simple and natural.

Pingue has managed to slow down time, taken the family traditions and kept them alive. The utmost care is taken by the Pingue family to offer consumers nothing but the best.

Based on some of my research, prosciutto is easily digested. Two slices of prosciutto contain six grams of protein, six grams of fat, and is a good source of energy. This particular type of meat is well within healthy choices we can make as consumers. As I always say all good things in moderation. The next time you're at the deli counter, give this particular meat a try, you will be pleasantly surprised and don't forget to ask for the locally produced prosciutto!

Proscuitto

Extraordinarily fantastic meat

Chipotle prosciutto wrapped chicken breast

PREP

Serves a family of 4-6
Prep time: 30 minutes
Cooking time: Approx. 25-30 minutes

INGREDIENTS

CHICKEN AND PROSCIUTTO

chicken breasts	4 washed
prosciutto	16-20 slices
paprika chipotle seasoning	sprinkle
rosemary	4 sprigs
sunflower oil	for veggies
arugula	2 cups

TOOLS

1 pot
1 frying pan
2 large roasting trays
1 large glass baking pan or
1 large cast iron pan
foil

TIPS

You can wrap duck, turkey and pork the same way with fantastic results. Try sweetening the dish up with apple-juice or pear juice, creating a salty sweet flavour.

Preheat oven to 375˚F.

CHICKEN PREP

Wash and slice each chicken breast into 5 two-inch strips along the short side. Roll them in the chipotle seasoning and wrap each slice in 2 pieces of prosciutto.

Tuck them neatly into an iron skillet, drizzle with sunflower oil and add 1 inch of water.

Lay the rosemary on top of the chicken wraps. Cover with foil and roast on the bottom rack for about 25 minutes.

If you like your proscuitto to brown a little, toss under the broiler for a few minutes at the end.

SEE NEXT PAGE FOR A GREAT WAY TO SERVE THESE PROSCUITTO WRAPS.

“Simple, fast and full of amazing flavors. This dish is easily served with all kinds of fresh in-season vegetables.”

Chipotle prosciutto wrapped chicken breast with fall veggies and mash

PREP

Serves a family of 4-6
Prep time: 30 minutes
Cooking time: Approx. 25-30 minutes

INGREDIENTS

GARLIC MASHED POTATOES

garlic	2-3 cloves
white potatoes	5-6 medium
soya milk	6-8 tbsp
sunflower oil	6-8 tbsp
garlic powder	sprinkle
sea salt	to taste

FALL VEGGIES

red peppers	2-3 sliced
yellow squash	2-3 small sliced
sunflower oil	drizzle
sea salt	sprinkle

TOOLS

1 pot
1 frying pan
2 large roasting trays
1 large glass baking pan or
1 large cast iron pan
foil

TIPS

Keep the juice from the baked chicken and pour it over the plated chicken. You can even add some of it to the mashed potatoes for that extra kick!

Preheat oven to 375˚F.

GARLIC MASH

Fry the garlic in sunflower oil on medium heat until crispy and light brown. Set aside.

Peel, cut up and boil the potatoes in salted water until soft and then drain the water. Mash the potatoes adding the sunflower oil, soya milk, a generous sprinkle of garlic powder and sea salt to taste.

The texture should be creamy and smooth. Mix in half of your garlic now and leave the rest for plating on top of the potatoes.

FALL VEGGIES

Wash and clean the insides of the vegetables and slice into ¼ inch thick rounds. Lay them on a baking tray, drizzle with oil, sprinkle with sea salt, cover with foil.

Bake the chicken and vegetables for 25-30 minutes. The chicken should be tender when poked. When one side turns brown, The vegetable rounds should be flipped to brown the other side. Bake just until they are cooked, and not too soft.

Plate the vegetables first as shown, fill the centre of the squash with mashed potatoes topped with fried garlic, and the chicken on some arugula or salad greens.

“Why not create shapes and colourful dishes. This makes eating much more fun for you and the kids.”

Fresh carrot and potato soup with peas

PREP

Serves a family of 4-6
Prep time: 5 minutes
Cooking time: Approx. 8-10 minutes

INGREDIENTS

large fresh carrots	4 whole
large white or yellow potatoes	2 peeled
medium cooking onion	chopped
sunflower oil	for frying
fresh parsley	3-4 tbsp
ground sage	pinch
sea salt	to taste
liquid chicken stock	4 cups
water	1 cup
fresh peas	1-1½ cups
GARNISH	
matchstick carrots	1 cup
organic pumpkin seeds	¼ cup
Disaronno®	few splashes

TOOLS

1 pressure cooker
(or large stock pot - cooking time will at least double)
1 small pot
1 frying pan
1 plate
hand held-blender

TIPS

It is a great idea to invest in a hand-held blender and a pressure cooker to reduce the time it takes to make soups. They allow you to keep the soup hot right in the pot while blending it.

Wash and peel the potatoes and carrots. Cut them into large chunks.

Cut the onion into slices and fry them in sunflower oil until they brown a little.

Toss the vegetables into the pressure cooker, (minus the peas,) and the seasonings. Add chicken stock and enough water to cover the vegetables.

Cover, set the pressure cooker on high, and cook for about 5 to 8 minutes.

In a stock pot, after 20 minutes, use the consistency of the carrots as your gauge.

While the soup is cooking, blanch the peas in salted boiling water, drain and set aside. When the soup is cooked, blend until nice and creamy, adding water to thin it if needed.

Add the blanched peas.

Using a hot frying pan, toss in the matchstick carrots and a few splashes of Disaronno. Reduce the liquid and set the matchstick carrots aside on a plate. Repeat the process with the pumpkin seeds.

Serve the soup and garnish each bowl as seen in the image. Really fun and simple!

This soup can be eaten hot or cold.

“Great tasting soups take very little time to prepare. Adding peas to a creamy textures makes for interesting eats!”

Sourcing whole natural grain-filled breads

There are several amazing bread makers and artisans alike in our area. We have some great choices when it comes to healthy bread.

What is interesting is that when travelling in the United States, the majority of the grocery stores are not carrying whole healthy breads; they are still carrying the less expensive soft white bread.

Locating a bread company with history, and being family owned was very important to me when sourcing a local supplier to talk to.

Stone Mill Bakery seems to be creating a whole natural line of bread products and I truly enjoy spending a little more to get the wholeness I'm looking for. It is still a family run business, boasting 100 years of European bread-making skills. They take pride in making the finest artisan breads and some of the most nutritional breads available in Canada today.

I had the opportunity to sit down with Gottfried in his bread making facility and talk about the importance of being a true artisan bread maker. He is very proud of the art behind the bread he makes and is in touch with nutrition and quality.

This seems to be missing in the majority of the commercial breads out there.

The key is to read the ingredients and really see if the grains are whole, if there is glucose and fructose and other really interesting ingredients that really are not part of a healthy diet. Really great breads are made from the simplest ingredients containing whole grains.

During our visit he told me he was in the process of changing some food ingredients in his breads, to accommodate food allergy concerns, specifically soy allergies. He felt by removing this he would be able to offer his breads to more consumers. I believe that he is really in touch with the customers' wants and needs and his bread recipes are loaded with nutritional whole grains, carefully stone milled into pure whole grain flour. As well he is using all natural and organic ingredients.

Really great breads are made from the simplest ingredients and whole grains.

One thing I found quite interesting about his bread making is that it's sprouting grains right in the dough before it is baked! How nutritional is that? For those who want a healthy tasting and completely nutritional bread, this is the one I would recommend. So next time you're in the grocery store instead of doing the pinch for softness test, just look for the one with the whole grains and ingredients that make sense.

Breads
with whole grains

Crunchy chicken cutlets on a pretzel baguette

PREP

Serves a family of 4
Prep time: 15 minutes
Cooking time: Approx. 4 minutes per side

INGREDIENTS

red and yellow peppers	2 sliced
baby spinach	4 cups
sea salt	sprinkle
tiny Spanish pearl onions	6 sliced
salad mix	2 cups
fresh dill	for garnish
chicken breasts	2-4
sunflower oil	for frying
sea salt	sprinkle
pretzel baguettes	4 fresh

COATING

white or whole wheat flour	½ cup
eggs	1-2
whole wheat or white crackers, salted	1-2 bags
dried oregano	1-2 tsp
garlic powder	1-2 tsp
fresh thyme	2 tsp

TOOLS

1 large frying pan
1 bowl for fried pepper slices
3 medium sized bowls for coatings
1 plate for coated cutlets
2 plates with paper towels for cooked cutlets

TIPS

Try using sunflower oil when frying; it takes the higher temperature and allows the full flavour of whatever is cooking to come through. Sunflowers are grown right here in Canada for oil. It is light and tastes great!

GARNISHES

I like to get the garnishes ready first, before the chicken, so you can assemble the sandwiches while the chicken is still hot.

PEPPERS

Slice your peppers into 2 inch slices. Fry on high heat in sunflower oil and set aside.

Wilt your spinach in the same pan, season with sea salt, and set aside. Slice your Spanish onions to have ready, alongside the salad mix and fresh dill.

CHICKEN

Wash and cut each chicken breast into 4 thin slices. Put the slices between plastic wrap and hit them with the tenderizer mallet until they are all very thin. Season them with sea salt and set aside.

PREP

Crush the crackers into tiny pieces by hand and season as listed above. You may need more or less crackers depending on how well you coat the chicken. Season the crackers.

Believe me; they make the crunchiest, tastiest coating, way better than bread crumbs.

Once you try this coating you will be hooked!

CONTINUED NEXT PAGE

“I wanted a coating that I could make for Anastasia without any traces of milk. Whole wheat crackers was the perfect solution as they make the crunchiest, tastiest coating.”

Crunchy chicken cutlets on a pretzel baguette cont'd

CONTINUED FROM PREVIOUS PAGE

Set the bowls in order, first the flour, then the beaten eggs, then the seasoned crackers.

Coat the cutlets one at a time - first with flour, then dip them into the eggs, then into the crackers and coat them nicely. Set each one on the plate until all are coated.

Start the frying pan on medium heat and pour a little sunflower oil on the bottom. Once it is hot, add the cutlets, three or more at a time, depending on pan size.

Fry until they are golden on one side; then flip over to cook the other side.

This may take 5-7 minutes depending on how thin you cut the chicken and how quickly your stove cooks.

You may need to adjust between medium and high heat. Once they are golden, put them onto a plate covered with a paper towel to absorb excess oil, until all are done.

If the oil looks tired or has too many bits of crackers in it, discard it, wipe the pan, and resume cooking with fresh oil.

Otherwise the next cutlets will not cook up as nicely or taste as good.

Cut the baguettes in half to serve your chicken cutlets on them open faced. Start with the wilted spinach, then the salad mixture, and then the cutlets, peppers and onions.

Toss on some fresh dill for that extra flavour.

"Making fresh cutlets is simple. You can prepare these the night before for your next day's lunch."

Pistachio chicken on spaghetti squash topped with sweet blackberries

PREP

Serves a family of 4-6
Prep time: 15-20 minutes
Cooking time: Approx. 45-50 minutes

INGREDIENTS

chicken breasts	4 skinless/boneless
spaghetti squash	2 large
sunflower oil	for frying
pistachios	1½ cups
flour	½ cup
sea salt	to taste
pepper	to taste
eggs	2 beaten
blackberries	2 packages
liquid honey	drizzle
rosé wine	dash
poppy seeds	½ cup
cane sugar	2 tbsp

TOOLS

1 pot
3 frying pans
1 baking pan
1 bowl
3 shallow dishes

TIPS

Try using walnuts or almonds for the coating; a great way to get nuts into your diet. Using various in-season fruits when cooking chicken creates new flavors for your family. Apricots, currants, gooseberries, raspberries or strawberries are great starters. Brandy and fruit wines also reduce nicely.

Preheat oven to 425°F.

Cut the squash into halves, clean them out, drizzle with sunflower oil and sprinkle with sea salt. Place in baking pan, cover with foil, and bake for about 45 minutes.

Wash the chicken breasts and boil in water for 15 minutes, until they are not pink inside. Drain and set aside to cool before coating them.

COATING

Put the flour seasoned with sea salt and pepper into a shallow dish. Beat the eggs in a bowl for the egg wash. Shell and crush (not too small pieces) the pistachios and put into a shallow dish.

First coat the chicken with flour, then dip in the egg wash and roll in the pistachios. Fry the chicken breasts with just enough sunflower oil on medium to cook the coating.

While cooking turn as necessary, about 15-30 seconds for each side, otherwise the coating may burn and lose colour. Remove from pan, split the top of each breast, set aside.

BLACKBERRY REDUCTION

In a frying pan, reduce the blackberries with one tablespoon of liquid honey and and a dash of rosé wine. Set aside.

In another small frying pan, toast the poppy seeds until they start to pop!

By now the spaghetti squash should be done baking. Pull it from the shells and mix the cane sugar and toasted poppy seeds into it, season with sea salt and pepper.

Plate the food as shown in image.

“Try using fresh in-season local fruits as part of your main dish. It creates interest, colour and definitely adds to the flavour!”

An education in free-range chicken farming

Let's talk turkey about naturally grown chickens, ducks, geese, quail and Cornish hens.

We have many local farms raising free range chickens, ducks, turkeys, geese, quail and Cornish hens. These birds are quite chatty and loud when they sense your presence. They are all beautiful creatures that should be raised with care.

Quotas play a role here, too, which limit the number of birds any one farmer can have. They also incur very high set-up costs. I do not see the need to repress the farmer and tell him what he can or cannot do in these cases. To me, it's like telling a pizza store owner they have a limit on the number of pizzas they are allowed to sell. Lock the door and go home! While we live in a democratic society, this is not what I am seeing when it comes to farming in North America.

I am very fortunate to live close to Everdale Organic Farms. They are an educational learning centre that has on site egg laying chickens, turkeys, a few cattle, and also grow their own vegetables all for sale.

What is really cool about their facility is they offer school programs to educate kids on farming and sustainable living. Farmers like this are offering incredible information for our kids to be in touch with the food that comes from the soil. I am certain that in your local community you can source learning centers like this.

We are in fact shrinking our own markets and allowing the import of animals that we can easily raise here. We can be rest assured, that the birds raised here are taken care of and are processed properly.

The real taste in food comes from the hands that raise it.

We can't verify what processes are used abroad. Try a fresh turkey from a local farmer next time you are cooking turkey; you will be quite surprised at how different it tastes from the store-bought variety. The same applies to all birds that are raised naturally. Eating chicken from a farm like Berretta is so noticeably different. The kids can easily identify with a better-tasting chicken.

I sometimes wonder what did chicken taste like 100 years ago. Did it look the same or has it been bred into something different? The real taste in food comes from the hands that raise it. I really enjoy watching the chickens intermingle with the turkeys, roaming free and pecking at the dirt for bugs. There is something very natural about letting nature take its place, giving the animals the freedom to grow.

The eggs are absolutely fantastic and are always for sale at the farm, fresh every day.

Poultry
raised naturally

Honey and thyme 'chick' on a bed of cous cous

PREP

Serves 4-6
Prep time: 20 minutes
1st Cooking time: Approx. 1 hour
2nd Cooking time: Approx. ½hour
Cooking times vary depending on the weight

INGREDIENTS

whole organic chicken	1 washed
local wine	1 bottle
apple juice	2 cups
Empire apple - chopped	1cups
cous cous	2-3 cups
cooking juices	2-3 cups
fresh garlic - chopped	6 cloves
curry, smoky paprika,	1-2 tsp of each to
garlic powder	be sprinkled
sea salt and pepper	to taste
fresh thyme	2-4 sprigs

SEXY SPICE - Make this separately, to use some now and save some for your next favourite dish!

curry	11 tsp
garlic powder	11 tsp
smokey paprika	3 tsp
sea salt	2 tsp
pepper	1-2 tsp

HONEY THYME - You can also prepare this ahead of time so the flavour of the thyme infuses into the honey. If you are rushed, just drizzle the chicken with honey at the end and you will get a similar taste.

fresh local liquid honey	½ cup
fresh thyme	2-3 sprigs

TOOLS

1 large roasting dish
1 bowl for chopped apples

Wash the whole chicken, and cut it up the spine, opening the chicken with meat side up, as in the photo. Place it in the roasting pan.

Sprinkle 6 tablespoons of the spice mixture all over the chicken. Add your beer and apple juice.

Put the chicken in the oven for about 15 minutes at 425°F to seal the skin, then cover with foil and roast at 350°F for about 1 hour.

Every chicken is different in size so you will need to gauge the final cook time based on what you see.

About 10 -15 minutes before it might be done, add your chopped apples and cous cous. If the liquid is low, add a cup or two of water. Continue to bake until it's ready to serve.

Drizzle honey thyme over the chicken just before serving. It is good to have some extra to drizzle at the table.

If you have not tried organic chicken, you really should. The taste is extraordinary, as is the moisture content of the chicken. To know if you are getting a fair price, look at the cost per pound.

I have found that sometimes the cost is exactly the same, but the organic chicken is typically twice the size. If a small commercial chicken costs $9.50 and the organic chicken is $18.00, check the weight.

In most cases I find that I am getting two chickens in one for the organic chicken!

Château des Charmes Estate Bottled 'Old Vines' Riesling
VQA Niagara-on-the-Lake

Riesling
Pinot Blanc- Alsace or Switzerland-
Klingenfus, Wunsch Mann or Caves d'Auvernier

"This one is meant to be fun and sexy ...besides it tastes really great. Why not spice things up a little in the kitchen!"

Sugar roasted ginger carrots

PREP

Serves 4-6
Prep time: 10 minutes
Cooking time: Approx. 30-45 minutes

INGREDIENTS

large carrots	5 peeled
brown sugar	¼ cup
fresh ginger	3 slices
maple syrup	¼ cup
sea salt	to taste
sunflower oil	drizzle
fresh parsley	garnish

TOOLS

large glass baking tray
foil

TIPS

You can overcook these carrots and they will taste even better, much like roasting peppers in the oven. Sometimes those little burnt bits taste the best!

Peel and slice up the carrots as shown in the image. Season them with brown sugar and large chunks of fresh ginger.

Drizzle with maple syrup and sunflower oil, then season with sea salt. Cover with foil and bake in the oven until cooked.

This dish goes well with roasted or barbecued meats. Often I will prepare vegetables like this just to eat as a snack!

“This is a recipe that my kids ask for often. How can you resist the simplicity behind this one? Quick and easy to prepare.”

Wasabi pea tuna steak on a bed of wild and scented rice

PREP

Serves a family of 4-6
Prep time: 10-15 minutes
Cooking times: Rice- Approx. 20-30 minutes
Tuna: Approx. 3-4 minutes max per side

INGREDIENTS

tuna steaks	4 3oz pieces
scented white rice	1½ cups
wild brown rice	1 cup
hot wasabi peas	¾ cup crushed
baby cucumbers	3-4 sliced thinly
fresh egg	1-2
sunflower oil	for frying
sea salt	to taste
avocado sauce	½ cup

TOOLS

2 pots for 2 types of rice
1 bowl for beaten egg
1 frying pan

TIPS

Tuna steaks can be a little pricey. To make it more affordable and get the perfect square, ask your butcher to cut them the size you want. Meals can get a little "same old" so spicing things up a little and trying new dishes will make it all the more enjoyable!

Château des Charmes Gewürztraminer,
St. David's Bench Vineyard,
VQA St. David's Bench

Gewurztraminer Riesling
Calamus Riesling, Niagara Ontario
or Dr Hermann Riesling Kabinett, Mosel Germany

Cook the 2 types of rice separately in advance, but keep warm for serving. This recipe calls for fluffy rice and wild rice.

Slice up the cucumbers with the skins on and set aside.

Season the tuna steaks with sea salt. Coat the edges of the tuna steaks with the beaten eggs and the crushed wasabi peas.

Fry the tuna steaks in sunflower oil on medium to high heat for 2-3 minutes per side.

Plate the wild rice first, add the sliced cucumbers, and then the white rice.

The tuna steak is laid on top with a dollop of avocado sauce.

This one will certainly impress guests at your dinner party!

“Sourcing local can be very challenging. Does anyone have a suggestion for a local wasabi pea supplier? ”

Adobo (chicken legs and potatoes in a pan)

PREP

Serves a family of 4-6
Prep time: 5-10 minutes
Cooking time: Approx. 40 minutes

INGREDIENTS

chicken legs	8 skin on
potatoes	6 large
spanish onion	1 large
sunflower oil	for frying
garlic	3 cloves
ginger	½ tsp
white vinegar	2-3 tbsp
soya sauce	a few shakes
brown sugar	4 tbsp
bay leaves	2 dry
sea salt	to taste
chicken stock	1-2 cups
water	2 cups approx.

TOOLS

1 large pot
1 bowl with water for potatoes

TIPS

This recipe is perfect for those busy ladies and busy guys who want to eat well without the fuss and the muss! All in one pot, with fantastic flavour!

Wash the chicken legs and score deeply on all sides to ensure cooking through. This is optional for those who are just beginners, not necessary if you have experience.

Peel and quarter the potatoes.

Chop the red onion and fry it in sunflower oil until it starts to caramelize. Add the chopped garlic and ginger and then turn the heat down to medium.

Add the chicken legs and vinegar and cook for about 10 minutes, stirring. Add the potatoes, soya sauce and brown sugar.

Add the chicken stock and/or enough water to cover the potatoes and chicken. Toss in the bay leaves and simmer for 35-45 minutes.

Do not taste the sauce until the potatoes and chicken are cooked. You can re-season at this time.

The sauce should be nice and brown, like the chicken has created its own gravy!

Adobo can be served with fresh vegetables, cabbage salad. Try my Sweet red cabbage and crunchy carrot recipe it makes a great side for this dish.

"This is both a traditional European/Philippine dish. It's all prepared in one pan, and is simply delicious!"

Orange pepper and fresh dill omelette

PREP

Serves 4
Prep time: 3-5 minutes
Cooking time: Approximately 5-10 minutes

INGREDIENTS

fresh eggs	6
orange pepper	1 sliced
fresh dill	a pinch
sunflower oil	drizzle
sea salt	to taste

TOOLS

1 large oven friendly frying pan
1 large mixing bowl

TIPS

Using the broiler helps those who are not omelette-flipping types. You may flip the omelette using a plate first and then return to the stove.

Preheat oven to broil for browning the omelette

Clean the pepper, removing the white flesh and seeds, and then slice it into strips.

Clean and tear apart the dill into small pieces.

Use a large stainless frying pan that you can transfer to the oven easily.

When cooking eggs, do not be shy with the oil or the omelette will stick to the pan.

Preheat the pan with oil in it, beat the eggs well in a bowl, and pour into the hot pan. Wait a couple of minutes and then turn it down to medium heat. Eggs taste better when they are gently cooked over medium heat.

Lay the pepper strips into the omelette and sprinkle in the dill.

Cover with a lid and cook for a few minutes, until the bottom is slightly browned.

Then transfer to the oven and broil until the top is also slightly browned. Remove from the oven and let cool for a few minutes.

Prepare toast or baguette, rye or whole grain—all go well with omelettes. Tastes great with a large serving of fresh garden vegetables.

“Omelettes are fast and simple to prepare. They are perfect for lunch and dinner, and can be made using fresh in-season ingredients.”

Quick and easy blueberry pancakes

PREP

Serves a family of 4-6
Prep time: 5 minutes
Cooking time: Approx. a few minutes per pancake

INGREDIENTS

whole wheat flour	¾ cup
all-purpose flour	¾ cup
vanilla sugar	1 packet
brown sugar	6 tablespoons
applesauce	½ cup
fresh egg optional	1
baking powder	1 tsp
baking soda	½ tsp
raspberry juice	½ cup
fresh blueberries	1 cup
sunflower oil	for frying

TOOLS

2 mixing bowls
1-2 frying pans, preferably pancake size to make cooking easier!

TIPS

My daughter's classmates love these pancakes with whole wheat and fruit. You can make them even more nutritional by adding flax or bran. Introduce a little at a time so the kids get used to the taste!

Wash the blueberries and cut them in half.

In a large bowl, mix applesauce and brown sugar, with the egg, until smooth.

Mix all other dry ingredients in a separate bowl. Whisk the dry ingredients gradually into the wet. Add the raspberry juice at this time, stirring until all the flour is mixed in & moist.

Put sunflower oil into the pan(s) and warm up on medium heat. This will give a crunchy texture to the pancake—kids love it!

Place the blueberries in the pan first, skin-side down. With a ladle, drizzle pancake mix over the blueberries, covering them slowly so they stay in place as you incorporate them into the mix.

Cook until tiny air bubbles appear—peek under the pancake to see if it's browned.

Flip the pancake and cook until golden brown on the other side.

Drizzle oil into the pan(s) between pancakes—to make them crunchy!

Cook one at a time (in 2 pans if you're fast!) and keep monitoring the heat. Sometimes you must lower it because the pan gets hotter the longer you use it!

You can create new flavours by using raspberries, fresh cherries, fresh strawberries and pairing them up with fruit juices of the same flavor.

The possibilities are endless and if you like nuts, this is great place to add to the recipe. If you are allergic to eggs, just add an extra teaspoon of baking powder.

"Try introducing fresh and whole wheat slowly. The kids say these pancakes rock!"

Toasted almond shortbread cookies

PREP

Serves 60 plus
Prep time: 5 minutes
Baking time: Approx. 9-10 minutes

INGREDIENTS

whole wheat flour	1 cup
all-purpose flour	1 cup
sea salt	½ tsp
toasted chopped almonds	1 cup
non-hydrogenated lard	1 cup
icing sugar	1/3 cup
brandy	1 tsp
almond extract	1 tsp
extra icing sugar	2 cups for coating

TOOLS

1 sifter
1 mixer
2 bowls
2 parchment sheets
2 cookie sheetsr
diamond shaped cookie cutter, 1 inch wide

TIPS

If you want to build a thicker coating on the cookies, hit them with the icing sugar while they are hot out of the oven! It tastes great and coats the cookies more. Do not let the cookies cool completely or the icing sugar will not stick.

Combine the first 4 dry ingredients in one bowl. In the other bowl, with the mixer, blend the lard and icing sugar. Once light and fluffy, add the brandy and almond extract.

Add your dry ingredients and mix only until the flour disappears.

Roll to about ¼ thick or less between two parchment sheets, cut out the cookie shapes, place them on the cookie sheets, and bake for about 9-10 minutes.

Make sure to cook them through. Even if they are a little brown, they still taste great!

Set on a cooling rack for 5-7 minutes and then sprinkle with icing sugar from the sifter while the cookies are still warm.

Personally, I have icing sugar in a bowl to drop the cookies into so the sugar is on all sides, and I finish them off by sprinkling the tops for the perfect presentation. Your guests will love them!

“It’s amazing how you can make a butter cookie without the butter. It tastes even better with natural ingredients. They are soooo yummy!”

Candied orange biscotti

PREP

Makes 24-30 cookies
Prep time: 5-10 minutes
Baking time: Approx. 45-50 minutes

INGREDIENTS

all-purpose flour	1½ cups
whole wheat flour	½ cup
ginger	1 tsp
baking powder	1 tsp
sea salt	½ tsp
non-hydrogenated shortening	½ cup
brown sugar	1 cup
eggs	2
vanilla	2 tsp
pure orange extract	1 tsp
candied orange preserve	½ cup
lemon rind	1 tsp

TOOLS

1 large bowl
2 large non-stick baking sheets
2 sheets of parchment paper

TIPS

These biscotti are light and have a texture like toast. If you like the more traditional biscotti, try my cranberry cardamom biscotti. They are both great!

Preheat oven to 375°F.

Mix dry ingredients together and set aside.

Cream the shortening with the brown sugar until smooth.

Add the eggs, one at a time, beating until creamy.

Add the vanilla, orange extract and keep mixing.

Add the dry ingredients and blend until the flour is completely mixed.

Now add your candied orange and lemon rind.

The mixture should become a little sticky. Turn out onto a floured countertop.

Divide in half—use a little flour so it does not stick to your hands. Create 2 logs, 1½-2 inches high, 4-5 inches wide, 9 inches long, rounded on top.

Lay them on parchment paper to prevent too much browning on the bottom.

Bake in the oven for about 30 minutes until golden.

Remove from the oven and let cool on the baking sheet for about 10 minutes.

Then slice off each cookie, about ¼ inch thick, with a sharp serrated knife. Lay the cookies directly on the baking sheets. (No parchment paper this time!)

Bake for 10-15 minutes per side, until they are golden and dry.

Take out of the oven and let cool.

“Each biscotti recipe creates a different type of cookie. This one is light like toast, and perfect for dipping in coffee”

Sustainable ways to use your water

Without water we do not survive. Shouldn't we all be aware of the water we drink?

In North America, because we can afford to, we drink water freely, and in most cases we waste it just as freely. We are so spoiled we actually pay to drink water from springs overseas thinking it is better than the water we have here. And in most cases we pay more money per litre than we pay for gasoline.

How much more local can water be than from your tap? Somehow we have been made to believe that it may be cleaner and healthier to drink bottled water. This is not true and is causing some serious damage globally. We are polluting the soil we walk on, the waters we rely on and seas that are so important for sustainability. To help control the amount of pollution and reduce plastic consumption we have many options available to us. Why not drink the the water from your tap? If it tastes funny or has an odour, call a professional to do a water test. Typically these problems have to do with high mineral and/or iron content. There are filters, filtration systems with simple solutions for these small problems. We should just be happy we have clean running water.

Since we all like to take water with us wherever we go, transporting fresh water is really simple and easy to do. Never mind the reduced cost and plastic consumption. So what we have done is gone out and bought stainless water bottles that are BPA-free.

I feel it is important that we give our kids positive ways to incorporate a healthier more sustainable lifestyle. Since water is so valuable to our existence, I felt it necessary to teach the girls the importance of water. For the kids I like to have colourful stainless bottles, that they can fill and reuse every day. We fill them up and use them as needed, always having extra ones in case they do get left at school or at friend's house. This is the easiest, most sustainable way to transport water without too much environmental impact. And fun too!

Water is only as precious as we believe it to be

If you are looking to reduce your carbon footprint immediately, this is a really quick, simple way to do so. Water is only as precious as we believe it to be, and this is one way we can protect and preserve one of the most important components of life.

There are many ways to modify our behavior without too much trouble. Making small commitments can be implemented slowly and added to one's daily routine.

How much more local can your own water source be?

Water

straight from the tap

White brownies

PREP

Makes one tray of brownies
Prep time: 5 minutes
Baking time: Approx. 30-35 minutes

INGREDIENTS

whole wheat flour	½ cup
all-purpose flour	½ cup
baking powder	¼ tsp
orange zest	2 tsp
ginger	1 tsp
sea salt	½ tsp
unsweetened applesauce	½ cup
sunflower oil	1 cup
cane sugar	1½ cup
eggs	4
BLUEBERRY REDUCTION	1½ cups
blueberries fresh or frozen	½ cup
honey unpasteurized	2 tbsp
cornstarch	

TOOLS

11 x 7 brownie pan
2 bowls
mixer
frying pan

TIPS

This is a perfect dessert that can be changed up with the seasons. Peaches, purple plums and apricots are all very easily worked into this recipe.

Preheat oven to 325˚F.

Combine the dry ingredients, except for the sugar, in a bowl and set aside.

Mix the wet ingredients—oil, applesauce and sugar, adding one egg at a time, and blend until creamy.

Add in the dry ingredients just to completely mix. Pour into a greased brownie pan.

Reduce the blueberries and honey in a frying pan for about 5 minutes, until the berries turn purple and start to break open.

Mix 2 tbsp of cornstarch with 2 tbsp of water and use to thicken the reduction. It should become thick, like a pie filling. Add a bit more if necessary.

Drop half the reduced blueberries by spoonfuls into the brownie mix before baking. Keep the other half of the reduction for the finished dessert.

Bake for 35 minutes on the middle rack, or until golden and a knife comes out clean.

Cool and cut the brownies.

Drizzle on the remaining blueberry reduction to serve.

“These brownies are a must, and will not last a day. I have taken the traditional brownie and made it a little healthier, with no dairy and no chocolate.”

Chewy chocolatey cranberry raisin oatmeal cookies

PREP

Makes 30-36 cookies
Prep time: 5-10 minutes
Baking time: Approx. 12-15 minutes

INGREDIENTS

brown sugar	1 cup
cane sugar	½ cup
whole wheat flour	½ cup
all-purpose flour	¼ cup
baking soda	1 tsp
ground cloves	2 tsp
cinnamon	2 tsp
nutmeg	1 tsp
sea salt	pinch
fresh egg	1
non-hydrogenated vegetable shortening	1 cup
water	4 tbsp
cocoa powder	½ cup
vanilla	1 tsp
orange zest	1 tsp
dried cranberries	½ cup
dried raisins	½ cup
rolled oats, large flake	3 cups

TOOLS

2 bowls
2 cookie trays
mixer

TIPS

These cookies can be made with a non-hydrogenated margarine to give you a chewy texture. Try adding walnuts and pecans. If you're crazy about nuts they taste great!

Preheat oven to 335°F.

Mix all the dry ingredients except for the rolled oats in a bowl and set aside. Measure the cranberries and raisins and set aside.

With a mixer, combine the egg, non-hydrogenated shortening, vanilla and orange zest.

Once it is creamy start adding the dry ingredients, but not the rolled oats.

Once they are mixed in, add the cranberries and raisins, and then the rolled oats.

Break the mixture into halves and add the cocoa and water to one half.

TO MAKE TWO-TONE COOKIES QUICKLY
Pinch a little batter from both bowls to form each cookie with your hands. Alternatively, take a teaspoon of each batter and press together on the cookie tray.

Leave a couple of inches between cookies as they will spread out.

Bake them for 12-15 minutes or until the lighter batter is golden. Remove from the oven and transfer to a cooling rack.

Repeat the process until all are cooked.

TO MAKE UNIFORM SPIRAL COOKIES
Roll the 2 batters out separately, same length and width, and then lay them together. Roll up and freeze for at least 2 hours.

Cut your cookies from the end of the roll and bake them the same as above.

“Chocolate cookies with no butter and no milk, that are packed full of fibre and goodness. All the reason to just eat more.”

Precious diamonds

PREP

Makes 48 cookies
Prep time: 10 minutes
Baking time: Approx. 15 minutes

INGREDIENTS

flax seeds	½ cup
whole wheat flour	2 cups
baking soda	1 tsp
baking powder	1 tsp
sea salt	½ tsp
crushed bran flakes	2½ cups
shredded coconut	2 cups
golden raisins	1 cup
non-hydrogenated lard	1 cup
brown sugar	1 cup
eggs	2
pure vanilla extract	2 tsp

TOOLS

small frying pan
2 bowls
mixer
2 cookie trays
parchment paper
1" wide diamond-shaped cookie cutter

TIPS

You may use all kinds of dried fruits for this one too! Dried blueberries, cranberries, cherries, or even toss in toasted raw organic sunflower seeds! As in all my cookie recipes you can use oil in place of the non-hydogenated lard if you choose.

Preheat oven to 345°F.

Toast the flax seeds in a hot, dry frying pan until they start to pop. Set aside.

Combine the flour, baking powder, baking soda and salt in a bowl and set aside.

In another bowl, mix the bran, coconut, raisins and flax seeds and set aside.

Cream the shortening and brown sugar. Add the eggs, one at a time, and beat until creamy, and then add the vanilla extract.

Add the flour mixture and blend it in completely before adding the bowl of bran, coconut, raisins and flax.

Use a diamond shaped cookie cutter sprayed with oil.

Pack the cookie cutter full of dough and push it out onto a cookie tray lined with parchment paper. Repeat until you have 8-10 per sheet as they do not expand much.

Bake them on the middle rack for about 15 minutes or until golden. Let cool completely.

Store in a glass cookie jar... if your family has not eaten them first!

“I have searched high and low for a great tasting cereal bar packed with fibre and nutrition but low in sugar. These are packed with toasted flax seeds, fruit, bran and whole wheat.”

Fresh, new sweet apple blossoms and buzzing bees

Spring. What does spring signify to you? For many of us it symbolizes a fresh new start with a little rain and warm sunshine! All the signs of spring are like a re-awakening.

The birds start to fly in and get busy. The tiny winter buds warmed by the new spring sun start to pop open with tiny new green leaves and the bees start to appear to do their wonderful job of fertilization.

All at once the landscape that was brown, starts to turn green, a unique fresh green that we see only once a year. If you're too busy to notice, take the time to look around at the change that takes place. It happens over a few weeks and is magnificent. What was once a grey forest full of empty branches quickly turns into a lush buzzing environment for deer, wild turkeys, birds and all sorts of tiny wildlife and insects.

This is a time to plant new plants and watch the farmers' fields dramatically unfold the seeds planted in late fall. Probably a winter wheat. It is a truly magical time of year and we are so lucky to be a part of it.

All around us farmers are planting outside crops with great anticipation for the best season ever.

This is a job where being an optimist is definitely a great asset. He and or/she is anticipating just the right amount of precipitaion, and the perfect amount of sun in order to reap the benefits of the land. They work very hard to produce the freshest, tastiest most nutritious foods for us to eat. Supporting local is key to a sustainable community.

I have found that bringing seasonal eating into my life, helps support my local farmer. They would like nothing more than for you to buy their crops when they are available at the local market and or local grocery store.

march • apples • potatoes • squash • beets • onions • cabbage • carrots • turnips • tomatoes • cucumbers • lettuce • mushrooms • parsnips • rhubarb • sprouts • sweet potatoes • peppers • **april** • apples • beets • onions • cabbage • carrots • turnips • tomatoes • cucumbers • lettuce • mushrooms • parsnips • rhubarb • rutabaga • sprouts • sweet Potatoes • Peppers • **may** • apples • carrots • turnips • onions • asparagus • spinach, cucumber • lettuce • Mushrooms • peppers • radishes • rhubarb • sprouts • sweet potatoes • tomatoes

Spring

blossoms are the begining

Spring asparagus wraps

PREP

Appetizers for 4-6 people
Prep time: 20 minutes
Cooking time: Approx. 20 minutes

INGREDIENTS

phyllo pastry	12 sheets
Ontario asparagus	12 washed
Pingue prosciutto	15-20 slices
garlic	for frying
sunflower oil	2 chopped
jalapeño pepper	1 chopped
garlic cloves	3 chopped
shitake mushrooms	6 chopped
sea salt	to taste
ground pepper	to taste
sunflower oil (for pastry)	¼ cup

TOOLS

2 cookie sheets
2 wire racks to go on cookie sheets

TIPS

Cooking tiny appetizers on a wire rack keeps the shape of the appetizer and prevents a leaky, sticky underside from forming while baking.

Château des Charmes Sauvignon Blanc,
St. David's Bench Vineyard,
VQA St. David's Bench

Sauv Blanc
Pinot Gris/Pinot Grigio
Klingenfus Alsace, Colli Vicentini Veneto Italy

Preheat oven to 350°F.

Rinse asparagus in cold salted water and clip off the ends; cut in half.

We are using only the tops for these appetizers so keep the other half for another recipe.
Set aside.

Seed the jalapeño pepper and chop it fine along with the garlic and shiitake mushrooms.

Fry them on high heat in sunflower oil until they are crunchy and brown. Set aside.

Lay out the phyllo sheets, oiling in between, in sets of three and cut each set into rectangular quarters.

On the phyllo, lay one slice of prosciutto (in the middle on an angle) and top it with fried mushrooms.

Add a stick of asparagus, placing it halfway up, also on an angle, so its tip is by a corner of the phyllo.

Fold the bottom corner of the phyllo up over the base of the asparagus before rolling the side portions tightly around it.

Repeat the process until they are all rolled. Wrap each with a ribbon of prosciutto as shown in the image.

Bake on wire rack for about 20 minutes or until golden.

“Sometimes the best things come in small packages. It's all about great tasting asparagus!”

Pastichio/macaroni pie

PREP

Serves a family of 4—6
Prep time: 30 minutes
Cooking time: Approx. 40-50 minutes

INGREDIENTS

ground lamb (or sirloin)	1½ lbs
onions	2 chopped
garlic cloves	2-3 chopped
sunflower oil	for frying
sea salt and pepper	for frying
fresh tomatoes	3-4 grated
white wine	1 glass
penne	900 grams
sunflower oil	¼ cup
eggs	3 beaten
toasted cornflake crumbs	1½ cups

(seasoned with fresh parsley, thyme, sea salt and pepper)

TOOLS

1 large frying pan
1 large pot
3 bowls
2 pots for béchamel sauce
1 large lasagna dish
foil

TIPS

Sirloin is a great substitute for those with more sensitive palates. This pie is well worth the effort, especially for those looking to tune up the "same old" macaroni dish!

Preheat oven to 400˚F.

Finely chop the onions and garlic and fry them along with the meat in a little sunflower oil, seasoning them with sea salt and pepper.

When the meat has browned, grate in the tomatoes, add the white wine, and simmer to reduce some of the liquid. Once reduced, set the pan aside.

Boil salted water and cook the penne for about 5 minutes, until tender. Drain and rinse the penne with cool water.

Put half in one bowl, half in another. Drizzle with sunflower oil and sprinkle ¼ cup of seasoned cornflake crumbs into each bowl. Beat the eggs and stir them in equally between the two bowls.

Mix one of the bowls of penne into the frying pan with the tomato and meat mixture.

Rinse the bowl that the eggs were in and then separate 2 egg yolks into the bowl to use later in the béchamel sauce.

START MAKING THE PIE
Sprinkle just over ½ cup of the remaining seasoned cornflake crumbs on the bottom of the lasagne dish and toss in some fresh herbs as listed above.

First, layer the dish evenly with half of the plain penne. Then cover it with all of the meat and then the penne and set aside for the sauce.

CONTINUED ON NEXT PAGE

"I love great Greek food! This dish is traditionally loaded with milk and cheese,but I wanted to create a lower calorie, dairy-free pastichio. So here it is!"

Pastichio/macaroni pie cont'd

PREP

Serves a family of 4—6
Prep time: 30 minutes
Cooking time: Approx. 40-50 minutes

INGREDIENTS

BÉCHAMEL SAUCE - This step should be done after the pie is assembled, so you can pour on the sauce and put the dish into the oven right away. If made ahead of time, the sauce will form a skin as it starts to cool, which we do not want to happen.

plain soya milk	4 cups
sunflower oil	6-7 tbsp
flour	7-8 level tbsp
sea salt and pepper	to taste
egg yolks	2 yolks only

CONTINUED FROM PREVIOUS PAGE

BÉCHAMEL SAUCE

Warm in one pot the soya milk. Heat up the other pot and put the sunflower oil into it.

Once the oil is hot, add the flour, one tbsp at a time, stirring with a whisk and cooking until it starts to brown.

Pour the hot soya milk gradually into the flour mixture—it will be very hot so it will boil and spit—be cautious as you are pouring and mix it steadily with the whisk. It should become like a cream sauce that will sit on top of the penne. Season it with sea salt and pepper to taste.

Remove from the heat and quickly stir in 2 beaten egg yolks. The sauce should be thick and ready to pour over the penne.

Pour the béchamel sauce onto the top layer of penne and sprinkle with the remaining cornflake crumbs.

Bake uncovered for up to 40 minutes, or until the top browns a little.

Cool for at least 30 minutes; otherwise when you cut the pie it will fall apart.

Cut into square pieces and serve with salad or on its own. This dish is incredibly tasty, almost addictive!

“For this dish I substituted milk for plain soya milk. It's just as creamy and full of flavour. We are not missing an ounce of great taste!”

Wild and scented rice with spinach and portabellas

PREP

Serves a family of 4-6
Prep time: 10 minutes
Cooking time: Approx. 35-40 minutes

INGREDIENTS

brown wild Canadian rice	1 cup
scented rice	1 cup
portabella mushrooms	5 sliced
fresh baby spinach	2-3 cups
sunflower oil	for fying
garlic	2-3 cloves
garlic powder	to taste
oregano fresh or dried	1 tsp
salt and pepper	to taste

TOOLS

1 large 15" frying pan with lid

TIPS

Try frying the ingredients first to bring out the full flavours in the dish. Often when frying mushrooms, I will fry them and set them aside to add to the dish at the end. This gives the mushooms a whole new taste.

Fry the mushrooms at a high temperature, turning them until they start to brown.

Add salt, pepper and oregano.

Add all the rice, chopped garlic and garlic powder. Fry for a few minutes to bring out the nuttiness in the rice.

Add water to cover the rice, by approximately 1 inch. You can add more later if you need to.

You may add the spinach now or when the rice is almost cooked. If you add it at this point, the flavours combine better.

Simmer on medium heat until the water almost disappears, turn the temperature to low, adding a little water if necessary, cover and let the steam finish cooking the rice!

It should be light, fluffy and very tasty!

These rice dishes are great for parties, barbecues and make great take-over dishes. Amazing for the kids' lunches.

A great side for chicken, quail, pork and beef.

"Simply adding the wild rice makes this dish nutritious, adds fibre, texture and enhances the flavour."

Simple family fun, enjoying fresh maple syrup

Maple syrup is an incredibly unique natural sweetner that is available in North America only once a year. The upper USA and central Canada are loaded with maple trees that produce the most amazing maple syrup. "This is our sugar of the North."

The girls and I collect maple syrup, boil it down and enjoy what we produce. We are not about to open a factory yet, but really enjoy the family fun we have around collecting the sap from the trees. Together we boil it down and fill up a few glass jars.

I am not sure what motivated Anastasia to start collecting the sap for syrup, but after many weeks of asking me to buy the tools I finally gave in. Every year now it has become a small tradition that we do not want to miss.

It was really quite simple to locate Jakeman's Maple Syrup Supplies. We placed a simple order over the phone and the box arrived the next day. We asked for three spouts, three buckets and three lids. It sort of looked like we all had our own personal bucket! And let's not forget the cloth-like strainer that catches the little friends that like to jump in for a taste.

Next we got their dad to drill the holes, insert the spouts and hang the buckets. What comes next is the watery syrup, that has almost no flavour. But wait until you start to boil it down, right on the stove top. At first it changes colour and starts to look a little cloudy, but you need to give it some time to reduce. Before you know it the maple syrup is boiling and shrunk to maybe a quarter of what you started with but you can tell something has changed. It smells really sugary and sweet. Within the season, the colour varies from the first sap collected to the sap collected many days later. Initailly the sap is light and somewhat golden. The sap thereafter darkens and becomes a different flavour.

The trees we tap are maybe 100-plus years old. The house is 150-plus so there is a possibility that they can be that old too. The syrup is fresh and has a nutty taste. This is not typical of store-bought maple syrup. I have yet to discover a similar one. It is really magnificent on pancakes, toast, French toast, drizzled on fresh fruit, and used as a reduction for nuts and fruit toppings. It creates a sticky goodness.

And for me, I love to use maple syrup in baking and roasting meats. It is "our sugar of the north" where the cold meets the warm sun and turns on the golden tap, drawing the sap from the roots of the maple tree up and out into our buckets.

Did you know that maple syrup has more calcium than milk by volume?

Nothing beats fresh homemade maple syrup!

Maple Syrup

Canadian maple syrup

PREP

Prep time: A day or more to collect a full bucket
Cooking time: Approx. 4 hours per pot

TOOLS

1 sap bucket with lid and 1 spout per tree
1-2 large cooking pots
glass canning jars/bottles
cheese cloth

TIPS

When you drill a hole in a maple tree, you must collect the sap until it stops running. Once the season is over, pull out the spout and plug the hole with soil to prevent ants and other problem-causing insects from entering the tree.

This is fun for the kids. You will not get a lot of syrup from one tree, but it is so fresh and tasty. Educational and fun with a delicious result—well worth it!

One bucket of sap will produce maple syrup to fill about ½ to ¾ of a small mason jar.

If you have a mature sugar maple tree, drill a hole to install the spout in March.

When the weather warms, the sap will drip, so hang the bucket with its lid on to keep out debris and intruders. You may need to hold it shut with a flat rock.

Have the kids check it carefully every day to see how much sap has been collected.

Once the bucket is full, bring it in and put the sap into a clean pot for boiling.

Hang the bucket back on the tree right away because once the sap starts to run, it does not stop for a few weeks.

It takes at least 4 hours to cook down one bucket of sap to become syrup.

Leave the lid off and boil the pot of sap on the back burner, away from the kids.

You will see the sap change colour as it boils down, eventually becoming golden and really bubbly while cooking—this is a sign that it is close to being done.

Spoon a little into a small, cold dish to do a taste test. This also let's you gauge the thickness of the finished syrup.

When you are happy with the flavour, turn off the stove.

Pour the hot syrup into a clean mason jar and allow it to cool. Then tighten the lid and store it in a cool place. Once you open it, refrigerate.

We did this and our first maple syrup was very nutty in taste, full of rich flavour, and golden in colour with a wonderful aroma.

It can be used in baking, or as a dip for fresh fruits, or poured onto desserts for that extra sweetness. The kids love the taste!

“Simply the best tasting maple syrup made in the backyard!”

Organic pumpkin seed and cranberry French toast

PREP

Serves a family of 4-6
Prep time: 5 minutes
Cooking time: Approx. 2-3 minutes per side

INGREDIENTS

Organic pumpkin seed and cranberry bread You can use French, Italian, rye, sourdough, or whole wheat!	1 loaf
fresh eggs	2-4
vanilla soya milk	2-3 tbsp
vanilla	1-2 tsp
sunflower oil	for frying
maple syrup	for drizzling
fresh strawberries	1-2 containers

TOOLS

1 bowl
1 non stick frying pan

TIPS

When making a meal that is mostly carbohydrates, add fruit and/or protein. This makes a more balanced meal that will also keep you full and more satisfied longer.

Slice your bread nice and thick ahead of time so it is ready, right by the stove.

Beat the eggs a little with a few tablespoons of soya milk and vanilla.

Put a slice into the liquid mixture while the frying pan is warming. Allow the bread to soak up the egg mixture on both sides, then lay it in the pan.

Cook on medium heat. When it looks golden brown, flip it! Judge by the crunchiness you want and flip it back over to get the desired look.

Repeat for each slice until all the French toast is cooked.

It is fun for the family to eat as the slices come out of the pan.

Drizzle with maple syrup and garnish with freshly sliced strawberries.

When the growing season changes, try using-blueberries, cranberries, currants, raspberries or gooseberries.

They will each create a new fresh flavor fit for the season!

"Sourcing a local artisan bread maker is just the begining of recreating a timeless favourite. Seeds and fruit add fantastic taste and texture, once you switch you'll never go back."

Spring rolls (Lumptia)

PREP

Serves 4-6
Prep time: 3-5 minutes
Cooking time: Approx. 7-10 minutes

INGREDIENTS

5 1/2 inch spring roll wrappers	**½-1** package
lean ground beef or pork	1 lb
carrots	1 cup chopped fine
celery	1 cup chopped fine
white onion	1 chopped fine
garlic cloves	3 chopped fine
eggs	2
crackers	½ cup crushed
sea salt	½ tsp
pepper	to taste
sunflower oil	for frying

TOOLS

1 bowl
1 frying pan
1 tiny bowl for water
wax paper
1 container for finished rolls

TIPS

Like phyllo pastry, spring roll wrappers can dry out if left open in the air too long, so it is always a good idea to keep a damp paper towel to cover the wrappers until you're ready to fill and roll. They can stay frozen for about one month.

Rinse the carrots and peel. Rinse the celery and remove the veins and peel the onion.

Then chop your onions, carrots and celery into tiny pieces. Do the same for the garlic and put into the bowl.

Add the meat, eggs, and crackers along with the seasonings and mix gently, but do not over mix or the meat will toughen.

Lay out your first wrapper, starting from a corner. It does not matter which one, then put about a tablespoon of the meat on the wrapper, form into a tiny sausage. Roll it halfway and tuck in both sides so the finished product looks like a sealed envelope.

Make sure they are tight so they do not come apart when frying. Dab your finger in the bowl with water to seal the loose end of the roll.

Place the finished spring roll into the container and repeat the process, laying them side by side, using the waxpaper to keep them from touching.

Keep out what you are going to cook and freeze the rest immediately for future use in an air-tight container.

Fry on medium heat in sunflower oil until they brown up nicely, 7-10 minutes. Turning them on all sides as they cook.

Break one in half to make sure they are fully cooked before removing.

"It can be great fun making food from other cultures. These are awesome little appetizers that can be prepared many days before cooking."

Asparagus is an extremely popular and versatile vegetable

In many parts of North America, as the seasons change, asparagus is growing. After a long, cold, yet beautiful winter, we are excited to see spring roll in, and wake up to a warm, sunny day that reminds us just how much we missed it.

The earth around us feels the warm sun too, and with the right number of sunny days, asparagus starts to make its way above ground again. The asparagus has been sitting dormant all winter long, waiting for the spring days to come and wake it up to produce fresh new tender green stems. In my area, it starts to grow in May, depending on the weather (give or take two weeks).

I think we all have a first fruit or vegetable of the season that we look forward to—the first crop that comes off the land. Many of us are unaware of how the imported asparagus is affecting our growers.

Often, when the home-grown asparagus is ready to ship to the grocery stores, the imports have beaten them to the punch, with lower prices to boot. Therefore, we are seeing the growers around our community starting to disappear.

I discovered this on my hunt for asparagus suppliers. When going to the grocery stores or the local markets, look for the locally produced varieties. It is one way that we as consumers can protect our local food sources and contribute to the local farmers. This has not been a concern for most of us based on my research as we seem to be shopping for food for price, size and quantity. In discussion with many of my peers, they are completely unaware of how their shopping habits are slowly narrowing our food choices.

> I think we all have a first fruit or vegetable of the season that we look forward to

It takes a few years to get fields of asparagus up and producing a decent crop and now we risk losing them to imports. Sounds like the car business in North America a little, don't you think? Consider where your asparagus is coming from and buy local.

So next time you're out buying groceries, which is probably in a few days, try to make a more valid decision about whose food you're going to buy.

It's all in our own backyard, locally produced, seasonally inspired and at the same time you will directly helping your local farmers and your community.

Asparagus

Rooting for healthy eating

Proscuitto asparagus wraps with thyme

PREP

Serves a party of 4-6
Prep time: 10-15 minutes
Cooking time: Approx. 5 minutes

INGREDIENTS

asparagus	2 bunches
prosciutto	300-400 grams
garlic powder	sprinkle

TOOLS

1 pot
1 BBQ

TIPS

When buying prosciutto, ask your butcher for locally produced meat. You will be amazed at the quality our local producers have for us. Also ask them to slice it for wrapping asparagus, and they will know how to slice it perfectly for you.

Preheat BBQ to 325°F.

Blanch the asparagus in boiling salted water for a few minutes, until it turns a rich green.

Remove from the water and let cool; sprinkle with a little garlic powder.

Wrap the prosciutto tightly around individual stalks of asparagus and eat them as they are, or toss them on the BBQ for that salty smoky taste!

Personally, I like the BBQ version; the meat gets a little saltier and the flavour makes its way into the asparagus!

Sourcing a nitrate-free, organic and naturally cured proscuitto was very important to me and my family.

"Try this one at your next party! Local, naturally raised and sulphite-free makes all the difference in how amazing these taste."

Fiddleheads with garlic

PREP

Serves 4-6
Prep time: 10 minutes
Cooking time: Approx. 5-10 minutes

INGREDIENTS

fresh fiddleheads	4-6 cups
garlic cloves	3-4 chopped
sea salt	to taste
sunflower oil	for frying
lemon	½ to 1 squeezed

TOOLS

1pot for blanching
1 frying pan for frying

TIPS

These are fantastic served together with cous cous, wild rice and goes well as a side dish for poultry fish and beef.

Soak the fiddleheads (ferns) in cool salted water. Wash them really well with a delicate hand—often they will be sandy.

Cut off the tail as sometimes it is a little brown. Start boiling the water while preparing the fiddleheads.

Blanch them in boiling water for about 3-4 minutes, remove and drain.

Fry the chopped garlic so it just turns a little brown and add the fiddleheads to the pan, season with salt and cook for a few minutes.

Slice up some fresh lemons, and set on the side of the plate, to be squeezed on just before serving.

These fiddleheads are available in the grocery stores in early spring, so if you would like to try them you need to keep your eyes on the vegetable section as the spring season is short.

If you're up to it they do grow wild in forests all around us, so you can pick your own "for free."

“Sometimes a local food is only available for a short time. When in-season foods are available, cook them up as soon as you can.”

Swiss chard, mushrooms and caramelized pecans

PREP

Serves a family of 4-6
Prep time: 10 minutes
Cooking time: Approx. 10 minutes

INGREDIENTS

swiss chard	1 bunch
white mushrooms	1 pkg sliced
pecans	½ cup chopped
ice wine	3 shots
sunflower oil	for frying
sea salt	to taste
ground pepper	to taste
lemon wedges	1 cut into ¼'s

TOOLS

1 pot
2 frying pans

TIPS

Try plating your greens in a new way to perk up your family's interest in eating them. Carmelized nuts give the salad a sticky and chewy texture. Fresh tender local greens always taste better than out-of-season produce.

Wash the Swiss chard in salty water, strain and chop into 1½ inch pieces or larger. Put into boiling water and cook for 5-10 minutes. Drain completely. Set aside.

Plate individually or on a serving platter. Drizzle with oil and sprinkle with sea salt.

Slice the mushrooms and fry them in sunflower oil on high heat, seasoning with sea salt and ground pepper while they are browning. More colour equals more flavour! Scatter them over the Swiss chard.

Toast pecans in a hot frying pan for 2—3 minutes. Remove from heat— pour in 3 shots of your favourite local ice wine, return to medium heat, and reduce until the ice wine forms a sticky coating on the nuts.

Sprinkle the caramelized pecans over the mushrooms and Swiss chard. Drizzle with lemon juice and serve warm.

Fresh, sweet, salty and so good for you!

"Swiss chard is one of the easiest greens to grow. and is packed full of flavour. These types of salads are perfect served warm."

Baby 'bellas with spinach and organic prosciutto

PREP

Serves 4-6
Prep time: 15 minutes
Cooking time: Approx. 3-5 minutes

INGREDIENTS

baby portabella mushrooms	24
baby spinach	4 cups
prosciutto	300-400 grams
sunflower oil	drizzle
sea salt and pepper	to taste
large green olives (optional)	6-12

TOOLS

1 frying pan
1 iron skillet or non-stick frying pan
1-2 serving trays

TIPS

Mushrooms are tender little things so these types of appetizers should be cooked and served right away, not made in advance. Socialize, cook and enjoy!

Clean the baby portabellas and remove their stems. Set them aside.

Wilt the spinach in a hot frying pan, drizzle with sunflower oil, season with sea salt and wilt.

Fry the baby bellas on high heat, searing them well to bring out the flavour. Do not over cook so they collapse, you want them to retain their shape and texture.

Lay them on their backs and drape the spinach over them as in the picture.

Add a nice slice of prosciutto and, as an option, top it off with a sprinkle of sliced olives. Fantastically delicious.

With its bold flavours, this is absolutely the best party appetizer. Full of rich flavours and absolutely fun to make!

"Why go frozen when you can go fresh? These fabulous appetizers are easy to make and are real show-stoppers!"

North American freshwater fish and fish farming

I have fond memories fishing with my dad at a very early age. I can remember how exciting it was to catch the first fish, return it to the water and start all over again with triple the excitement anticipating catching the biggest fish of the day!

Freshwater fish are a part of a North American tradition. Catching fish is part of an exciting sport, where you catch the fish for size and return it unharmed, back to the lake. Some people fish for the fun of it and others are extremely competitive, fishing for the trophy of their dreams. It is all in great fun!

Fishing was a part of my life as a child. Along with my brother and two sisters, we not only caught fish, but caught the bullfrogs and brought them home to our pond. We're not talking tiny frogs here; bigger than a large grapefruit! It is not an expensive hobby for the family and can be a lot of fun and very relaxing.

Freshwater fish are also raised on fish farms in our local communities. They are usually open to the public and are really interesting places to visit. I sourced Silver-Creek Aquaculture, a local fish farm and got together with Lou Maieron, and his wild Swan. Lou's Aquaculture is located right at the source point of the Credit River. Three springs erupt from the earth at about 600 to 1,000 gallons combined per minute. This source provides a steady flow of fresh water for Lou to have a very well productive and well stocked fish operation.

Lou, like any other producer, works hard and loves what he does without compromise. He is a master in his field with several ponds, one running into the next and the water is crystal clear, teaming with many varieties of freshwater fish. In one pond he may have bass, walleye, carp, koi and minnows. In another, rainbow, brown and speckled trout.

Really great food begins when we start to notice where it comes from

All of the fish are raised for sale to the public and may cost anywhere ranging from \$2-4 per fish. That is a really fair price for fresh fish in today's market. This fresh fish went straight from the water to my table. Need I say, "how fresh is that?"

I know it may sound a little odd, but we tend to place more value on our clothes, cars, and the things we "feel" we need. Our food is precious.

Really great food begins when we start to notice where it comes from, how long the journey was from the farm to the table, and if it was cared for with love and respect while it was being raised before we have the opportunity to buy it.

Fresh Fish

from water to plate

Crunchy flax trout with sprouts and wild rice

PREP

Serves 4
Prep time: 10 minutes
Cooking time: Approx. 30 minutes

INGREDIENTS

RICE	
wild rice	1 cup
scented rice	½ cup
garlic powder	½ tsp
sunflower oil	drizzle
CRANBERRY REDUCTION	
cranberries	1 cup frozen
maple syrup	¼ cup
brown sugar or Disaronno	¼ cup
FISH	
trout	1 rinsed and skinned
sea salt	sprinkle
dried tarragon	1 tsp
egg	1 beaten
organic flax	6 tbsp
sunflower oil	for frying
garlic cloves	2 chopped
BEAN SPROUTS	
bean sprouts	5 cups
sea salt	sprinkle
fresh dill	¼ cup chopped

TOOLS

1 small pot for rice
1 small pot for cranberries
1 small bowl for egg wash
2 plates for coating fish
1 frying pan for fish and sprouts
1 plate for cooked fish

TIPS

Timing is everything when cooking a dish like this, so take the time to prepare everything before you start - this makes it really easy.

Rinse and boil both types of rice together for 15 minutes in salted water. Reduce heat to low, cover, and steam for 5-7 minutes. Stir in garlic powder, a drizzle of oil, and set aside.

Slice the rinsed, skinned trout into 1-1½ inch pieces; set aside.

Boil cranberries in another pot with maple syrup and brown sugar (or Disaronno), while coating and cooking the trout.

Season trout with sea salt and tarragon, dip one side into egg wash, then into a plate of flax and set on another plate, flax side up.

Fry the trout on medium heat in sunflower oil and chopped garlic, flax side down first, for 3-3½ minutes per side. Set aside on clean plate.

Wipe the pan with a paper towel, drizzle with sunflower oil, put back on medium heat, toss in bean sprouts and sea salt.

Fry for a few minutes until sprouts start to go clear, and finish off with fresh dill.

Your cranberries should now be reduced to a nice sticky sauce; turn them off and set aside.

Plate as shown, Your family will be most impressed with the taste and textures you have created.

Château des Charmes
Estate Bottled Cuvée d'Andrée Rosé,
VQA Niagara-on-the-Lake

Rose Riesling
Calamus or Viewpointe Late Harvest- German Spatlese Dr Hermann, Weingut Martin Kerpen

"Fresh local fish can be prepared in many different ways. We really enjoy the crunchy flax coating and the soury sweetness of the cranberries."

Sweet crunchy red cabbage with carrots

PREP

Serves a family of 4-6
Prep time: Approx. 15 minutes

INGREDIENTS

red cabbage	1 large
Spanish onion	1 large
carrots	4 large
sunflower oil	1 cup
white vinegar	¼ cup
brown sugar	½ cup
sea salt and pepper	to taste

TOOLS

2 large stainless bowls with lids
food processor or lots of cutting patience!

TIPS

I personally like to cut the cabbage by hand, but you can use a food processor to speed up the process. Either way this is a tastier, low-calorie version of and old favorite!

There are no rules when it comes to how much sugar or salt in this salad, so be flexible and create your own taste. This recipe was created for the way my family likes it.

Slice up the cabbage nice and thin and divide it into the two bowls.

Do the same with the carrots and the onion.

Put half of the sunflower oil, vinegar, and brown sugar into each bowl and toss!

Salt and pepper to taste. This salad will last in a closed container for up to one week.

A perfect cool and refreshing salad for fall barbecues. Toss in some sunflower seeds walnuts or dried cranberries.

"It is amazing how addicitive a salad can be when you intermingle sweet with sour."

Skinny fries

PREP

Serves a family of 4
Prep time: 5-10 minutes
Cooking time: Until they are golden brown!

INGREDIENTS

potatoes	4-6 peeled
sunflower oil	2-3 cups
sea salt and fresh herbs	sprinkle

TOOLS

1 large deep pot
1 large bowl with cold water
1 plate with paper towel

TIPS

Try using sunflower oil; it is light, tasty and does not overpower the potatoes! Great for the kids or as an appetizer for your next party. You can easily use a slicer for the potatoes or a food processor to cut down the time.

This is where you get to really use your potato peeler—not just to peel the skin, but to peel the whole potato including the skin! It must be done by hand to get the skinny look that I am sharing with you!

Clean and wash the potatoes thoroughly. Then peel them completely, layer by layer, into skinny slices. They will fry up fantastic.

Let them soak in cold water until you are finished. Drain them in a colander and rest on paper towels to get the water off. It is very important not to have cold water hitting hot oil!

Deep fry them in sunflower oil, about a handful at a time, dropping them individually into the oil so they do not stick together.

Use a metal strainer or spoon to move them around so they brown evenly.

When they are golden, set them on paper towels to remove excess oil. Sprinkle with sea salt and fresh rosemary or thyme.

These fries are an absolute favourite of the kids, big people like them too!

"Thanks to the potato peeler, we now have skinny fries! Thin and crispy, these little fries are complete perfection."

Baked Swiss chard calzone

PREP

Serves a family of 4
Prep time: 10 minutes
Cooking time: Approx. 20-30 minutes

INGREDIENTS

Swiss chard preferably red	1 bunch
green onions	3-4
white onion	1 large
red chili pepper	1 small
fresh tomatoes	2 grated
fresh garlic cloves	2-3 cloves
sunflower oil	drizzle
fresh basil leaves	handful
sea salt and pepper	to taste

TOOLS

1 frying pan
1 large pizza pan (not vented)

TIPS

Brushing the calzone with oil gives you a crunchy brown crust that everyone will enjoy without deep frying!

Preheat oven to 400°F.

FILLING
Chop 2-3 fresh tomatoes into chunks.

Fry the chopped onion and garlic and add the tomatoes and spices. Simmer so that the flavours combine into the sauce.

Wash and chop the Swiss chard and green onions. When the sauce is ready, add the Swiss chard and green onions.

Season to taste. Remove from heat and let it cool a little.

CALZONE
Drizzle a little sunflower oil onto the pizza pan. Roll out the pizza dough to the size of the pan and place it there.

Pour the cooled ingredients onto one half and fold the other half of the dough over.

Pinch the dough to seal it well and brush with sunflower oil.

Bake on low rack for about 20 minutes; longer if it needs more browning.

PIZZA DOUGH SEE PAGE 206 FOR RECIPE

“I like to make a calzone that is large enough for the whole family, simple and easy! You can stuff the calzone with just about anything. This one is perfect for the vegetarian in you!”

Wild about locally grown Canadian rice

Sourcing local food products has never been easier. Choosing to cook with a local rice/grass vs. imported white rice is one way we can support local and get a more nutritious product. The upper USA and Canada are teaming with wild rice.

Murray Ratuski, from Shoal Lake Wild Rice, runs the family business that has been around for more than 70 years in Canada. This is important to me when searching for local food because I find that family businesses tend to have a genuine love for the products they produce, grow and sell.

What is interesting about wild rice is that it is actually grass (you would never know the difference); a very tasty grass. It grows on the shores of freshwater lakes.

Producers harvest their wild rice in various freshwater lakes in Ontario, Manitoba, Saskatchewan and Quebec in the fall.

> Wild rice is high in fibre, Vitamin B6 and has no sodium. The kids love it!

It is grown naturally and is hand-picked and roasted to perfection. As each season passes, the next crop may not be in the same lake as it was in the previous year. It may even appear in a lake that did not have a history of having rice growing in the previous year.

Because this rice is not grown in a field and is found naturally, it makes cultivating it much more of a challenge. This contributes to the higer cost of the rice. One way to offset the cost of a really great nutritious food is to use it sparingly with scented or basmati rice. It complements all of my dishes, adding texture and nutty flavours. I like to mix it in with white rice when cooking; wild rice is high in fibre, Vitamin B6 and has no sodium. The kids love it!

Sourcing wild rice suppliers is really easy to do. There are several here in Canada and all over the USA. So why is it we are so interested in eating rice from around the world when we have some of the most amazing rice right here in our own backyard? Supporting local growers and producers is going to help protect our wonderful food environment here at home.

We can promote our own good health and longevity through natural food, sourcing local, eating fresh and reading labels.

Wild rice or wild grass is part of the North American landscape, it is part of our culture, and land we live on.

Enjoy and try new healthy unique foods.

Wild Rice

Going against the grain!

Spanish rice with ground sirloin

PREP

Serves a family of 4-6
Prep time: 10 minutes
Cooking time: Approx. 30 minutes

INGREDIENTS

ground sirloin	1½ lbs
spanish onion	1 chopped
jalapeño pepper	1 chopped
garlic	2-3 cloves
black eyed beans	1 can with liquid
scented or brown rice	1½ cups
wild Canadian rice	1 cup
sunflower oil	for frying
fresh oregano (or dried)	2-3 tsp
garlic powder	sprinkling
sea salt and black pepper	to taste

TOOLS

1 large frying pan

TIPS

When cooking rice dishes, cover the rice with just enough water and continue to add 1/4 cup at a time allowing it to boil away. Cook for about 25 minutes, turn the stove to low, cover and let the steam do the rest. This will help you get the perfect rice that separates easily and does not stick. Be careful as you add water to the rice—if you add too much, you cannot take it back out.

Chop up the Spanish onion into small pieces and fry in sunflower oil until golden.

Add finely chopped jalapeño pepper and minced garlic into the oil with the onion. Cook until they start to caramelize.

Add the ground sirloin and fry until brown, also adding the spices to taste.

Add the scented rice and the wild rice; cover with water.

Stir in the black eyed beans.

Boil gently until the water starts to cook down, making sure you add a little at a time to completely cook the rice.

Scented rice should be fluffy and gently fall apart, with the flavours infused from the sirloin and the jalapeños!

Wild rice should be firmer, creating a nutty amazing taste along with really great texture.

This is the perfect rice dish for any occasion. It goes well both with pork and chicken.

“I decided to take a Spanish rice dish and tweak it just a little bit, using ground sirloin, tossing in wild rice to give it a more local appeal.”

Potato cuties!

PREP

Serves a family of 4-6
Prep time: 10-15 minutes
Cooking time: Approx. 5 minutes to caramelize the onions and 3-5 minutes per appetizer

INGREDIENTS

white potatoes	4 grated
Spanish onions	1-2 sliced
sunflower oil	for frying
fresh oregano leaves	for accent
garlic powder	sprinkle
fresh thyme	a few sprigs
sea salt	to taste
fresh arugula	1 cup

TOOLS

2 large frying pans (ceramic)
paper towels

TIPS

You can always top these little ones off with fresh fried salmon bits or tiny slices of prosciutto.

Grate and soak the potatoes in cold salted-water for about 5 minutes. Drain them and season with fresh herbs, garlic powder, and sea salt.

Slice and fry the onions on high in sunflower oil until they are browning and caramelized. Set them aside on a paper towel.

Put sunflower oil into 1 or 2 frying pans. Heat them up to medium. Make sure the potatoes are well drained. Season.

Pinch the amount you want. A tablespoon or so will make a nice sized appetizer. I use my fingers to select the right amount, and gently place 3 or 4 in each pan.

Do not flatten the cuties too much; they need a little air and thickness to look good. Cook on one side until it turns golden; flip and cook the other side.

Stoves cooks differently, so you will have to adjust your heat accordingly. For the best taste, quickly wipe the pan and refresh the oil between batches. When cooked, place them on a paper towel.

Once everything is cooked, assemble the appetizers: Sweet potatoes first, followed by the arugula, and then the caramelized onions. Top with fresh oregano!

IF YOU ENJOY THIS ONE, TRY THE SWEET POTATO CUTIES ON PAGE 278

“Everyone loves tiny little tasty appetizers that are packed with flavour. These little cuties are simple, fresh and easy to prepare, so enjoy!”

Finding time to stop in at local markets and farmers' markets

I love market shopping—it is a very relaxed and a stress-free way to take your time, select your food and create your menu based on what is in season. If your local area does not have farmers' markets try to find a grocery store that supports local producers by carrying their products. You will enjoy the whole grocery shopping experience that much more!

Everyone loves a relaxed shopping experience. I am not sure that much enjoyment can be had if you're shopping for food where you cannot move and take your time to select the best foods for yourself and or your family.

Why not be a grocery store connoisseur, and demand nothing but the best?

I enjoy shopping at different markets while I am out and about. I have found some really great places to shop that support local and carry some of the finest fresh fruits, vegetables, organic chickens, beef and pork. Not to forget the fresh locally made breads!

When in need of groceries, and I'm on the road I like to stop in at markets along the way. I consider this to be a green way to shop. You can supplement your regular visits to your local hometown grocery store in search of new and interesting foods. This will inspire you, as it does me, to create new recipes, and source new flavours.

From the start of spring until the end of Autumn I can be found in a variety of local markets, farmers' markets and small grocery stores outside my immediate neighbourhood.

I frequently stop in to see my friend Mike at one of his locations, Oak Ridges Food Markets or Concord Foods, and always pick up groceries when I am there.

We have so many shopping options along our country roads. Rock Garden Farms, a beautiful countryside market run by Margaret and her husband Paul, has a stunning display of in-season foods, garden plants and hanging baskets. When I am passing by, I'll stop in to pick up some fresh produce.

When Muscovy duck or locally grown meats are on my list, I pop in to see Janine at Broadway Farm's Market.

Why not be a grocery store connoisseur, and demand nothing but the best?

We have at least three farmers markets within 30 minutes of our house—great places to enjoy on the weekend with the kids.

When going grocery shopping, spice things up a little and try stopping in at one that you've never tried before. Not only can it be very convenient, but you will have gained yourself an entirely new shopping experience.

Local Markets

shopping conveniently

Greek inspired roasted potatoes

PREP

Serves a family of 4-6
Prep time: 5-10 minutes
Cooking time: Approx. 45-60 minutes

INGREDIENTS

baby potatoes white & purple	2 containers
sunflower oil	¼cup
chicken soup base	1 tsp
chicken stock (water an option)	½-1 cup
oregano fresh or dried	sprinkle
garlic powder	sprinkle
paprika	sprinkle
sea salt	to taste

TOOLS

11 x 15 glass pan
foil

TIPS

This is one of the best kept family secrets for roasting potatoes. Add at leat one inch of liquid, usually water to the potatoes, cover and roast. The water will eventually disappear, toss under the broiler and you will have the best roasted potatoes ever!

Preheat oven to 425°F.

Wash and lay the potatoes in a single layer in the baking pan without overlapping them.

Drizzle sunflower oil generously over the tops of the potatoes. Sprinkle soup base and all spices on the potatoes. Pour the water on the sides, without disturbing the seasonings.

Cover with foil and roast for roughly 45 minutes to 1 hour, or until slightly crunchy and the skins are browning.

Roast the potatoes for the last 15 minutes without the foil to get that crunchiness on the outside. It may take a little longer depending on the oven.

If they are cooked but still need browning, turn on the broiler, move the pan up to the top rack, and broil for a few minutes until you get the desired colour.

“Everyone wants to know the secret behind the perfect roast potatoes. Roast them with water and they will be moist on the inside and crunchy on the outside.”

Taste the difference of fresh local lamb

It was really nice to get out and meet a farmer who nurtures his lambs and clearly has a bond with them. The nature of the connection between farmer and animal is lost between the consumer and the product we see in the grocery store.

There seems to be a real disconnect between the food we buy and where it comes from naturally. Taking the time to visit local farms and having the kids see where the food is reared is natural and very important. I am very concerned that a lot of kids are unaware that the food they are eating is over-processed and lacks the nutritional value of naturally grown food. We need to reconnect our children with real food.

Interestingly enough, on our visit to nearby Bert's Lamb, my kids and I had arrived to see baby lambs just barely a few minutes old. They were thrilled and very excited to see how soft and beautiful they were. I was interested in how Bert raised his lambs and found out that he raises them as naturally as possible to keep the meat antibiotic-free, free of anything unnatural. He is increasing production this year as the farmers' markets are getting busier and people are becoming more interested in eating fresh local lamb.

It seems that there are issues for our local lamb producers as imports are being used to fill the high demand for lamb, leaving no room for our local farmers to compete.

What is becoming increasingly more popular is mutton, which is a mature sheep, passing one year of age or having a baby. The meat is quite different than lamb, but if cooked right and seasoned well, it makes quite a tasty dish.

Apart from their meat, the wool that these animals produce is incredibly warm and soft. It contains a waxy lanolin which makes the wool somewhat waterproof and is a natural fire retardant. It would be very uplifting if we could see this used more in our clothing today instead of polyesters.

> There seems to be a real disconnect between the food we buy and where it comes from naturally.

Raising sheep and lamb presents a great opportunity for our "green" university students who are looking for a more relaxed career in farming. North America needs local farming to be revived in order to create a sustainable economy and help keep food prices down. Farming is cool, and should not be overlooked when choosing a career.

Farmers' markets and specialty stores are a great place to get fresh local lamb.

Spring Lamb

Maple balsamic Ontario lamb chops

PREP

Serves 4
Prep time: 15 minutes
Cooking time: Approx. 7-10 minutes for the lamb
Cooking time: Approx. 3-5 minutes for the veggies

INGREDIENTS

ONTARIO LAMB CHOPS	12 washed
balsamic vinegar	2-4 tbsb
sunflower oil	drizzle
brown sugar	¼ cup
garlic cloves	4 chopped
Ontario Boston lettuce	1 head
CURRY SWEET GRATED CARROTS	
large carrots	2 grated
sunflower oil	for frying
brown sugar	¼cup
sea salt	to taste
curry	sprinkle
SPICY RED BELL PEPPERS	
red bell peppers	2 sliced
sunflower oil	for frying
jalepeno pepper	1 sliced
dried chilies	sprinkle
sea salt	to taste
GINGER SWEET PEAS	
frozen sweet peas	2 cups
sunflower oil	drizzle
ginger	sprinkle
MAPLE GLAZE	
maple syrup	½ cup
brown sugar	¼ cup

TOOLS

BBQ
2 frying pans
2 pots
resealable container for marinating

Preheat BBQ to 400°F.

Clean and slice the peppers, grate the carrots, seed and finely chop the jalapeño, and measure the peas, keeping them all separate.

Start by boiling salted water in one pot. BBQ the lamb chops 3-4 minutes per side until cooked to your liking. Remove and set aside.

In boiling water, blanch the peas for 3-5 minutes, while frying the other veggies.

On medium to high heat, fry the carrots in sunflower oil for a couple of minutes, add brown sugar and season with salt and curry.

Fry only a few more minutes and remove from heat. Repeat the process with the peppers, adding the jalapeño, chilies and season with salt. They should only take a few minute as well. Remove and set aside.

In a small pot, heat up the maple syrup and brown sugar and let boil until it starts to reduce and get sticky. Remove from heat.

Serve on top of the Boston lettuce as shown in the image. Drizzle the warm maple glaze over the lamb chops and enjoy!

When preparing vegetables like this, the cooking time is kept to a minimum, keeping all the full flavours, colours, and textures to make the veggies come alive!

Château des Charmes Pinot Noir,
Paul Bosc Estate Vineyard,
VQA St. David's Bench

Pinot Noir Malbec
Valdivieso Single Vineyard Malbec- Chile,
A good Argentine Malbec over $15.00

“Spring is a sign that fresh local lamb is ready for the barbecue. Try making your own sauces from natural ingredients like maple syrup and balsamic vinegar.”

Warm Swiss chard and potato salad

PREP

Serves a family of 4-6
Prep time: 5-10 minutes
Cooking time: Approx. 30 minutes

INGREDIENTS

potatoes- yellow or white	6-8
Swiss chard	1 bunch chopped
sunflower oil	to drizzle
sea salt	to taste
fresh basil	¼ of a bunch
fresh garlic (optional)	1 clove chopped
fresh green peas (optional)	1 cup

TOOLS

1 large pot for boiling
1 large bowl for serving or you may choose to plate individually

TIPS

Try planting Swiss chard in the garden this year. It will last until the snow falls and produce for the whole season, tender and fresh, every day!

Wash and peel the potatoes. Cut them into wedges, 4 or 6 depending on the size of the potato.

Wash and cut the Swiss chard into small pieces. Set aside.

Always add potatoes to already boiling water. Boil the potatoes halfway and then add the Swiss chard to avoid overcooking it.

Continue boiling both potatoes and Swiss chard together until potatoes are tender.

Drain the water and bathe the potatoes/chard in sunflower oil.

Add chopped garlic (optional), sea salt and herbs to taste. For a sweet taste, add some fresh green peas.

The potatoes should be a little green and taste like Swiss chard—wonderful!

“Why not try this lower cal version of potato salad? It’s excellent when the Swiss chard is available in early spring, so fresh; simply delicious!”

Margeritza Greek Easter soup

PREP

Serves a family of 4-6
Prep time: 30-40 minutes
Cooking time: Approx. 30 minutes

INGREDIENTS

lamb spleens	2 washed
lamb hearts	2 washed
lamb sweet breads	2 washed
sunflower oil	drizzle
green onions	2 large bunches
dill fresh	½ cup
sea salt and ground pepper	to taste
romaine lettuce	1 chopped
scented rice	1 cup
egg yolks	3
egg white	1
lemon juice (freshly squeezed)	1 cup
flour	3 tbsp

TOOLS

2 bowls
1 pressure cooker (8 litres)
OR — 1 large stock pot
1 soup ladle
mixer

TIPS

This soup takes a little patience but is well worth it. Find a local lamb producer (farmers' markets are usually the best bet) for specialty meats that you may not find so easily at the grocery store.

Put the rice into a bowl of water to soak for 15 minutes.

Boil the lamb organs in half a pot of water for about half an hour, removing any foam. Strain the liquid into a large bowl through a paper towel.

Cut the lamb organs into 1 inch chunks. Fry them in the pot/pressure cooker in sunflower oil until the meat is browned. Then add the onions and sauté.

Add the liquid back to the pot with the meat and onions. This gives you a nice clear soup. Add your freshly chopped dill, close the lid, and set to cook under pressure for 10 minutes. (20 minutes or more if using a stock pot.)

Cool off the pressure cooker, safely remove the lid and continue cooking.

Add sea salt and ground pepper to taste, then the thinly sliced romaine, top up the pot with water. Cook uncovered for another 10 minutes.

Rinse the rice, add it to the soup, and bring it to a boil uncovered over medium heat. Continue cooking untilt the rice is tender.

Beat the eggs well, adding the lemon juice to them. Gently add 3-4 soup ladles of the hot liquid to the egg/lemon mixture and beat it together. This prevents the egg from forming into visible pieces. Add the mixture to the soup, stirring until mixed.

To make the soup a little thicker, mix 3 table-spoons of flour with ¼ cup of water and add it to the soup, stir in. The soup should look rich and creamy. Enjoy!

“We all have a favourite traditional food. It happens that this one has become an everyday family favourite. An absolutely sustainable dish.”

Enthusiastic for elk!

These days we are on the lookout for something unique without giving up good nutritional value in what we buy. Grocery stores tend to sell mainstream meats and I wanted to venture out and meet up with a natural elk farmer.

I met Anthony and his wife at Black Willow Elk Farm and spent some time with Anthony walking the ground where the elk grazed naturally. This is another family business that has been operating free range for about five years and deserves to be recognized as a unique local meat supplier.

The elk are fed natural grains and are pastured and taken care of with respect in a stress-free environment.

What intrigued me was the relationship Anthony had with his animals. As with other farmers I have met on my food jouneys, he has a real connection with the animals he is rasing. In fact, most if not all of them, had names. To me this seemed very cool.

Like any good farmer, Anthony believes in only using natural products and refrains from using antibiotics unless the animal's health is threatened. So he has a quaint little farm where he raises his elk. When they're ready for slaughter he sends them out to a certified facility, where they also produce elk sausages, as well as various other cuts of meat.

This particular meat tastes amazing and is everything you want in a meat - easy to cook, moist and tender with a wonderful taste. When you're looking for something different than the everyday meat, try elk. It is just as nutritious as beef and as tender as veal.

I like the fact that elk meat is not being mass produced. It is a very different looking meat with almost no visible fat and takes very little time to cook. If your're looking for a healthier alternative for everyday beef, elk meat may be the one your looking for.

You can buy fresh elk in the form of tenderloins, sausages (mild, Italian and spicy) and cuts that you would find similarly to beef. You will have the best chances sourcing elk at local farmers' markets or at a specialty grocery stores.

Be adventurous and try sourcing meats that are untouched by large commercial farming facilities in your local area. You will be pleasantly surprised at what exists beyond the grocery store.

The elk are fed natural grains, pastured and are taken care of with respect in a stress-free environment.

Elk
a leaner choice

Elk skewers with yellow zucchini, garlic and thyme

PREP

Makes 8 large skewers
Prep time: 10-15 minutes
Cooking time: Approx. 10-15 minutes

INGREDIENTS

elk sirloin	2 lbs
yellow zucchini	2 cut into cubes
red peppers	2 chuncky slices
garlic cloves (whole)	12 cloves whole
garlic powder	sprinkle
fresh thyme	1 bunch
sunflower oil	for marinate
sea salt	to taste
fresh ground pepper	to taste

TOOLS

BBQ
1 container for elk
bamboo skewers—soaked overnight in water

TIPS

Try soaking your bamboo skewers so they will not burn or dry out the meat while cooking. I find when cooking very lean meats on the BBQ it is nice to have some oil, fresh lemons or marinade to keep them moist and juicy. Keeping the flame on medium also will help.

Preheat BBQ to 325°F.

Cut the elk meat into chunks. Marinate in the refrigerator in sunflower oil and garlic powder for 2 hours or overnight. This is just for flavour infusion, as elk is very tender.

Cut the zucchini and red peppers into cubes. Oil them so they stay moist while cooking, and season them.

Alternate the meat, garlic cloves, zucchini and red peppers on the skewers, wrapping them with the thyme sprigs and seasoning with ground black pepper.

Grill them on the BBQ on medium heat for 10-15 minutes, turning the skewers as they cook until done to your liking. Squeeze fresh lemons directly on the skewers while the are cooking on the BBQ.

These skewers are perfect for outdoor entertaining and offer your guests a fresh new dish that is simple and exceptionally tasty. The kids love colourful foods, especially from the BBQ!

“Sourcing a local and naturally raised meat such as elk was easy to find close to home. Animals that are allowed to graze naturally produce a meat that is full of flavour.”

Three green pesto

PREP

Makes enough for a week
Prep time: 5 minutes
Cooking time: none

INGREDIENTS

fresh dill	½ bunch
fresh parsley	½ bunch
garlic cloves	4-6 whole
sea salt	to taste
lemon juice	a few splashes
sunflower oil	1 cup
green onions	3 whole

TOOLS

1 food processor
1 container for pesto

TIPS

When making any pesto use your best judgement.Taste between mixing and adjust accordingly. You can toss in some fresh chilies or 1/2 the jalepeño to spice it up if you like. The taste is yours.

Simply delicious and absolutely easy.

Toss all your ingredients into the food processor and blend until the garlic is chopped up.

Taste as you go and adjust the seasoning according to what you like.

Pestos are simple and created based on your personal taste. Have fun and enjoy the simplicity of a great pesto!

They typically last for at least a week, usually two, and can be used with meat dishes, dipping for veggies and on toast in the morning.

“This is one of the easiest ways to create flavoured oils that are perfect for meats and dipping your favourite bread into. Natural and simply delicious!”

Beautiful, sweet, tasty in-season strawberries

I don't know anyone who will say 'no' to fresh, juicy strawberries. It seems that everyone loves their strawberries.

Due to contstant demand by consumers, some farmers are using growing techniques that are really off the wall. Strawberries are being chemically grown, gassed so they last during long transportation periods, and then shipped around the world for you and I to eat.

No doubt you have seen these fruit. They are obviously artificially big, really have little taste and can last in the fridge for a week or so. Typically when we pick fresh local strawberries they may last a day or two.

When we buy in-season strawberries, although they are noticeably smaller, they are fabulous! If they are natural and not coated in preservatives, they will not have a very long shelf life. Not that that is a problem because you will eat them right away!

The good news is that I am aware that some local farmers in the Niagara Region are producing strawberries right up until we get snow. I understand that they are being produced naturally with unique natural farming techniques.

We also have a local grocery store in my community that supports local strawberry farmers by buying the strawberries they produce over their extended growing season.

I am excited to see farming changing to accommodate our desire for fresh products by utilizing natural and organic techniques.

When we buy in-season strawberries, although they are noticeably smaller, they taste fabulous!

This way we may actually be able to protect our local food sources and have access to really great produce.

Strawberries are a beautiful fruit that we all love to eat fresh and use in our baking. Using them within their season allows you to enjoy their fresh sweet taste that typically comes once a year.

This being said, leaving them behind at the end of their season and moving on to the next locally produced fresh fruit is really not a bad thing.

This will allow you the opportunity to experience the next fresh fruit that will be available at your local grocery store or farmers market. You may be pleasantly surprised at teh variety of other fresh foods available for you to choose from.

What is even better is that when the strawberry season rolls in again the next year, your fond memories of how sweet and tasty last season's strawberries were gives you all the more reason to enjoy them all over again.

Strawberries

Organic, fresh, juicy and healthy

One big strawberry tart

PREP

Serves a family of 4-6
Prep time: 5-10 minutes
Baking time: Approx. 40 minutes

INGREDIENTS

1 portion of Salty cardamom short-bread dough

STRAWBERRY FILLING

strawberries	1½ cups
lemon juice	1 tbsp
cane sugar	2 tbsp

STRAWBERRY DRIZZLE

strawberries	½ cup
honey	½ cup

TOOLS

1 small pot
1 hand held blender
I large baking tray
2 sheets parchment paper

TIPS

Almost all tarts leak. This ensures a moist, juicy filling. You can always use plums, peaches, nectarines and small berries for this recipe. Keeps you in the season!

Preheat oven to 350°F.

STRAWBERRY FILLING
Wash, stem, and quarter the strawberries. Mix them with the lemon juice and sugar.

Roll the dough in an 8-9 inch circle, between parchments, to desired thickness.

Use the bottom sheet of parchment to lift the dough onto the baking tray. Pour the strawberry mixture into the centre, about 2 inches away from the edge. Using the parchment, push up the dough around the berries to create the pie shell.

Bake on the middle rack for 25 minutes. Take the pie out of the oven and pour over strawberry drizzle, then return to oven to finish baking.

STRAWBERRY DRIZZLE
Reduce the strawberries and honey in a pot and cook for about 5 minutes. Remove from stove and set aside.

Blend with a hand held blender. At the 25-minute mark, open the oven and drizzle onto the open tart. Close the oven and finish baking for 15 minutes more.

Because this dough is partially whole wheat it will not brown up like white dough, so remove at 40 minutes. You can also set it under the broiler for a few minutes as well to brown it up.

SEE SALTY CARDAMOM SHORTBREAD DOUGH RECIPE ON PAGE 360

“I find tarts make the most fun, simple and fantastic desserts. This is a great way to use in-season fruits.”

Kids' chocolatey strawberry stars!

PREP

Makes 12-15 stars
Prep time: 15 minutes
Cooking time: Approx. 20 minutes

INGREDIENTS

all-purpose flour	1½ cups
whole wheat flour	¼ cup
baking powder	2 tsp
baking soda	1 tsp
ginger	1 tsp
brown sugar	2 cups
water	2 cups
non-hydrogenated shortening	6 tbsp
cocoa powder	2 cups
eggs	3
vanilla	2 tsp
apple juice	¼ cup
strawberries	15
ICING	
icing sugar	1 ½ cups
sunflower oil	2-4 tbsp
hot water (plus extra to make thin)	2 tbsps
vanilla	1 tsp

TOOLS

2 large bowls
1 medium bowl
1 small bowl
1 large frying pan
2 small frying pans
whisk
star shaped cupcake trays
(usually 6 per tray)

TIPS

Utilizing in-season fresh fruit for toppings on cakes helps cut the calories without cutting out the sweet delicious desserts!

Preheat oven to 350°F.

Mix your dry ingredients in one large bowl. Set aside. In a small bowl, beat the eggs.

In the large frying pan, add the brown sugar and water and stir on medium heat until the sugar is dissolved. Turn off heat, add the non-hydrogenated shortening and whisk.

Once melted, whisk in the cocoa completely and then the beaten eggs. Last but not least, don't forget to whisk in the vanilla and the apple juice!

Pour the chocolate mixture into the empty bowl. Then add your dry ingredients and mix completely.

Spoon into oil sprayed trays (or cake pans) and bake for about 20 minutes or until an inserted knife comes out clean. (Cake pans may take up to 10 minutes more.) Cool on wire racks.

In a small pot, mix the icing sugar, sunflower oil, hot water and vanilla. Heat and cook for about 5 minutes and set aside to drizzle on cooled cakes.

Wash the strawberries in cold salted water, remove stems and slice the berries as shown in the image.

“Kids love shapes and moist chocolate cake! Who says you can't make a great tasting chocolate cake without butter, cream or milk?”

Strawberry salty stars!

PREP

Serves a family of 4-6
Prep time: 10-15 minutes
Baking time: Approx. 15 minutes

INGREDIENTS

1 portion of Salty cardamom shortbread dough

walnuts	½ cup
amaretto	3 shots

STRAWBERRY REDUCTION

strawberries freshly picked	1-2 pints
brown sugar	2 tbsp
maple syrup	¼ cup
fragoli strawberry liqueur	½ cup

TOOLS

2 frying pans
hand held blender
rolling pin
star shaped cookie cutter
2 cookie sheets

TIPS

I would suggest making these the day you want to eat them. The fresh strawberries will eventually soften the cookies. They probably will not last long anyway as they taste great!

SEE SALTY CARDAMOM SHORTBREAD DOUGH RECIPE ON PAGE 360

Preheat the oven to 335°F.

Wash all of the strawberries and cut out the stems. Pick out the best 24-30 to top the cookies and set them aside.

Cook down the remaining strawberries with brown sugar and maple syrup for about 10 minutes, add the strawberry liqueur, and reduce until moist but not watery.

Purée to dipping consistency and set aside to cool. It should be thick enough to coat the strawberries.

Roll the dough to ¼ inch thick, cut out the stars, and place on cookie sheets and bake them for 15-20 minutes, or until they start to change colour.

Remove from the oven and cool on a rack for about 15 minutes.

Dip the fresh strawberries into the strawberry reduction and place one on each cookie.

Put the chopped walnuts into a hot frying pan for 1-2 minutes. Remove from the heat for a minute and then add 3 shots of amaretto.

Return to low heat and simmer for a few minutes, then turn to high to reduce the liqueur until the walnut chunks are sticky. Turn off the heat and let the walnuts cool.

Gently stick the coated walnuts to the tops and sides of the strawberries.

Almost a tart, but more than a cookie!

“A delicious new cookie that revolves around a fresh fruit—salty sweet, and fun for the kids!”

How simply sweet local organic honey can bee!

In every province and every state in North America there are beekeepers, producing unpasteurized honey, liquid honey, beeswax candles and collecting pollen. Bees aid in the fertilization of crops and are contracted from time to time to help pollinate fields to ensure that the absolute best crops are in place for the coming season.

Honeys are very unique in taste and texture depending on where the honey is collected. We have many beekeepers in our area as you probably do, too.

In my local area there are a number of honey producers, some produce organic honey while others do not.

Truly organic honey that is federally certified, is by far the best honey for taste and health benefits. I found this interesting and ended up getting to know Dan and Nina Garyfalakis of Hockley Valley Honey Farm. You can see that they really love their work by the passion they have for it. Taking care of hives, keeping them pest-free, breeding his own bees, and producing one of the finest honeys I have ever tasted.

They use no antibiotics or chemicals and keeps his bees in isolated areas within a three-kilometer radius foraging area, creating a buffer zone clear of any fields contaminated with herbicides, pesticides, chemical fertilizers and genetically modified crops. He is located within the protected boundaries of the Niagara Escarpment where his bees pollinate from uncontaminated wild flowers.

They also use natural processes to collect the honey, with no heat used and or pasturization. The process is long, creating some really great tasting and creamy honeys.

Another beekeeper in our area, Randy Leitche of Leitche's Honey, produces his honey from his hives placed on local farms. His aim is to help polinate them, and he also collects the honey and uses similar processing techniques as Dan. He also produces a wonderful unpasturized honey.

We need bees to be healthy and productive for the future as the average lifespan of a worker bee is 35-45 days. If we interfere with nature's process, we risk the future health of the bees that we so heavily rely on.

Awareness will help you make better choices when buying the foods that are so precious to us today.

Truly organic honey that is federally certified, is by far the best honey for taste and health benefits.

Honey
organically delicious

Honey and maple syrup clove cake

PREP

Makes one large cake
Prep time: 10 minutes
Baking time: Approx. 45 minutes

INGREDIENTS

whole wheat flour	1¼ cups
all-purpose flour	1¼ cups
baking powder	2 tsp
baking soda	1 tsp
cinnamon	2 tbsp
ground cloves	3-4 tbsp
eggs	6
cane sugar	1½ cups
sunflower oil	1 cup
lemon	1
cognac	¼ cup
unsweetened applesauce	½ cup
gingerale	1 can

SYRUP

maple syrup	2 cups
water	½ cup
honey	¼ cup

TOOLS

2 bowls
1 medium pot for reduction
1 bundt pan

TIPS

If you let the cake cool, the syrup will not be absorbed as it should. Be sure to pour the syrup on while it is still hot. The taste is absolutely wonderful!

Preheat oven to 375°F.

Combine all of the dry ingredients, but not the sugar, in a bowl.

Beat the eggs on high speed, adding the cane sugar, sunflower oil, lemon juice and cognac.

At medium speed add the dry ingredients a little at a time, alternating with the applesauce and adding the gingerale, until completely mixed.

The mixture should be watery. Pour into a greased bundt pan.

Bake for about 45 minutes, or until a knife comes clean.

SYRUP

Just before the cake is done, make your syrup by reducing the maple syrup, water and honey.

When the cake comes out of the oven, while it is still warm in the pan, pour the syrup over it.

Turn it out of the pan as soon as the syrup is absorbed.

“This family recipe shared by Niki was given an update by bringing in whole wheat, maple syrup and cane sugar. And a whole lot of spices.”

Cranberry cardamom ginger biscotti

PREP

Makes 24-30 cookies
Prep time: 5-10 minutes
Baking time: Approx. 1st bake 30 minutes
Second bake 15-20 minutes

INGREDIENTS

all-purpose flour	1 cup
whole wheat flour	1 cup
cardamom	1 tsp
ginger	1 tsp
baking powder	½ tsp
sea salt	½ cup
non-hydrogenated shortening	1½ cups
brown sugar	2
eggs	1 tsp
almond extract	1 tsp
amaretto	1-2 tsp
lemon rind	1 cup
dried cranberries	

TOOLS

1 large bowl
2 large non-stick baking sheets
2 sheets of parchment paper

TIPS

If you're like me and want to cut the cookies without waiting the 10 minutes to cool down, give it a try. It changes the texture slightly and I personally find it easier to cut through.

Preheat oven to 345°F.

Mix your dry ingredients in a bowl and set aside. Start to prepare your wet ingredients.

Cream the shortening with the brown sugar until smooth.

Add the eggs, one at a time, beating until it becomes creamy.

Add the almond extract and amaretto and mix.

Add all the dry ingredients and blend until the flour is completely mixed.

Now add your lemon rind and cranberries. The mixture should become a little sticky.

Turn out onto a floured countertop. Divide in half—use a little flour so it does not stick to your hands.

Create 2 logs, 1½-2 inches high, 4-5 inches wide, 9 inches long, rounded on top. Lay them on parchment paper to prevent too much browning on the bottom.

Bake in the oven for about 30 minutes until the cookies are golden.

Remove from the oven and let cool on the baking sheet for about 10 minutes.

Slice each cookie, about ¼ inch thick, with a sharp serrated knife.

Lay the cookies directly on the baking sheets. (No parchment paper this time!)

Bake for 10-15 minutes per side, until they are golden and dry. Take out of the oven and let cool.

really like cardamom mixed with cranberries this dense biscotti. It's a cookie that is fragrant d naturally sweet.”

Summer is full of sweet fruits and tasty vegetables

Summer is really a fun time of year for everyone. The kids are out of school, and spring's first crops have been had and we look forward to what summer will produce for us.

This is one of several good reasons to take a trip to your local farmers' markets. Keep your eyes open at the grocery store and enjoy the tasty local produce that is available to us. The Niagara Region is by far ahead of most of Ontario's producing season, supplying us with the freshest most nutritious fruits and vegetables available.

Looking around you, you will see the fields full of fresh fruits and vegetables.

Take the kids out to local farms to pick your own strawberries! There is an appreciation that comes with knowledge that can be shared so easily with family and friends. Eating in season and local supports your community and your neigborhood farmers.

This is truly the end of a very beautiful beginning and the start of new season.

june • strawberries • cherries • green Beans • cucumbers • peas • cauliflower • broccoli • cabbage • radishes • turnips • lettuce • oni ions • spinach • green onions • garlic • kale • apricots • cherries • mushrooms • snow peas • peppers • radicchio • hubarb • sprout s • sweet potatoes • tomatoes • **july** • apricots • peaches • plums • blueberries • raspberries • sweet corn • green beans • snow pe as • cabbage • carrots • turnips • onions • radishes • beets • peppe rs • lettuce • spinach • celery • swiss chard • zucchini • potatoes • bl ue berries • red and black currents • gooseberries, mushrooms • snow peas • peppers • radicchio • rapini • raspberries • plums • rutabaga • sprouts • sweet potatoes • **august** • apples • apricots • peaches • plums • sweet corn, green beans • cabbage • carrots • turnips • onions • radishes • celery • swiss chard • potatoes • go oseberries • rapini • sprouts • eggplant • plums • grapes • leeks • musk melon • nectarines • parsnips • pears • squash • asian veg

Summer

A flavour-packed season!

Twisted sticky apricot chicken skewers

PREP

Serves a family of 4-6
Prep time: 10-15 minutes
Cooking time: Approx. 10-15 minutes

INGREDIENTS

chicken breasts	4-6
local honey	¼ - ½ cup
homemade apricot jam	1 cup
ginger	1 tsp
sea salt	to taste
saffron	to sprinkle

TOOLS

1 plate
6-8 metal reusable skewers
pastry brush
BBQ

TIPS

Experiment with pork, beef or chicken, and twist up your skewers with fresh fruit or last year's preserves. This is one way to keep it local and in season!

Château des Charmes Estate Bottled Late Harvest Riesling, VQA Niagara-on-the-Lake

Riesling Calamus Late Harvest, Ontario,
Dr Herman Urziger Wurzgarten Spatlese, Mosel Germany

This one is really a lot of fun!

One way to kick up a skewer in the early spring is to get out last season's jam and use it to coat the meat while cooking on the BBQ - sticky goodness, with all the rich flavours of last season's fresh fruits. The jam coating tastes just as bold as the day I made it.

Start by slicing the chicken into long strips, seasoned with sea salt and ginger. Twist and wrap them around the skewers and set on a plate while the BBQ heats up.

The best, most tender skewers are cooked slowly at a low temperature, this helps retain the moisture and not dry out the meat. This gives you plenty of time to socialize.

In a small bowl mix the honey and apricot jam together. Start to apply the mixture after the skewers have been on the BBQ for at least 5 minutes, coating the strips to make them nice and sticky.

Cook until the chicken is white throughout, up to ten minutes total. This will depend on how thickly your strips are cut. Keep the flame on low.

The more honey and jam mixture you apply, the stickier and sweeter they get!

“I love sticky chicken! This is a fun and simple way to get the whole family eating fruit in a whole new way!”

Fresh rapini with lemon, garlic and sunflower oil

PREP

Serves a family of 4-6
Prep time: 5-10 minutes
Cooking time: Approx. 3-4 minutes

INGREDIENTS

fresh rapini	2 bunches
fresh garlic cloves	2 chopped
sunflower oil	drizzle
fresh lemons	2 large
sea salt	to taste

TOOLS

1 large pot for boiling
1 frying pan
1 large bowl of cold water

TIPS

Almost all greens can be prepared the same way. This is a great way to prepare quick and easy nutritious snacks a day ahead. Something easy to grab from the fridge when you get home from a busy day at work.

Soak the rapini in salted water for 5 minutes.

Rinse off the rapini and cut off the bottom ends. Cut into two pieces, leaving a nice stem to go with the flower.

Put into salted boiling water for 3-4 minutes, until the rapini turns dark green. Remove from the hot water and dip into a bowl of cold water to stop the cooking process.

After 2 minutes, drain off the water and place the rapini on a large plate.

In a frying pan, heat up the chopped garlic in sunflower oil on low for a few minutes to get the garlic flavours out.

Drizzle the garlic-salted oil over the rapini. Add sea salt and squeeze a fresh lemon over the rapini just before serving. Choosing to wait will keep the rapini fresh and not change colour.

“Try eating lots of greens. These veggies are youthful and full of antioxidants. So quick and easy to prepare. Quicker than the drive thru.”

104
128
34
356
270
260
212
70
168
106
152
78
304
192
330

254
324
26
188
38
148
352
144
204
296
240
180
346
100
52
142
170

Crunchy pan seared broccoli with orange bell peppers

PREP

Serves a family of 4-6
Prep time: 10 minutes
Cooking time: Approx. 3-4 minutes

INGREDIENTS

fresh broccoli	2-4 heads
fresh orange peppers	2 sliced
chicken soup base optional	1 tsp
sunflower oil	for frying
sea salt	to taste

TOOLS

1 frying pan
1 serving bowl
1 colander

TIPS

We tend to make decisions for our kids and think they will not like vegetables made fresh and simple. Make sure you do not cook them too long as they continue cooking once removed from the pan.

Clean the peppers, removing the white flesh and seeds, and then slice it.

Clean and cut the broccoli into small pieces, including the stock and soak in salted water for 5 minutes.

Heat the oil in the frying pan, while the brocoli is draining in a colander.

Salt the oil lightly, add soup base for additional flavour, and fry the broccoli on medium to high heat, just until it turns dark green. Toss in the peppers for a few minutes, to start cooking them and remove from heat.

Season again if necessary, turn into a beautiful bowl and serve. Cooking vegetables this way keeps all the nutritional goodness inside, nothing gets lost in the water.

Broccoli like this is great for barbecues, parties, and as an after-work snack. Trying to use colorful veggies this way—it gets the kids more interested in eating them.

“Cooking fresh vegetables without water makes them even more colourful and appetizing. Keeping it fresh and simple means everyone may just eat more.”

Fresh broccoli, leek and pea soup

PREP

Serves 4-6
Prep time: 5 minutes
Cooking time: Approx. 8 minutes in a pressure cooker
Cooking time: Approx. 20-03 minutes stove top

INGREDIENTS

medium onion	1 sliced
garlic cloves	2 chopped
sunflower oil	for frying
salt and pepper	to taste
medium potatoes	3 peeled
broccoli heads	3 cut into peices
large leek	1 sliced
chicken stock	4 cups
water	up to 2 cups to thin
peas (fresh or frozen)	1½ cups
prosciutto	2-3 slices
baby spinach	1-2 cups

TOOLS

1 large stock pot (or pressure cooker)
1 small pot
1 frying pan
hand-held blender

TIPS

Try using a pressure cooker (if you have one) when making soups. Cooking under pressure reduces the cooking time and enhances the flavour. I also like to add chunks of other vegetables, giving the soup a creamy but chunky texture.

Clean, peel and chop up the potatoes. Wash the broccoli. Wash and slice the leek.

Clean and slice the onion. Chop the garlic cloves. Fry the onion slices and chopped garlic in a little sunflower oil, right in the pressure cooker or pot, until they are almost ready to brown. Season with sea salt and pepper.

Add the potatoes, broccoli and chicken stock. Cook under pressure for 8 minutes or, if using a pot, simmer until the potatoes are soft.

Use a simple hand-held blender to blend the soup right in the pressure cooker! Add water, if needed, to thin the soup a little. (If using a pot, sit it in the sink to blend the soup as it is very hot.)

In a small pot, blanch the peas so they are just cooked; only takes a few minutes. Drain them and add to the soup.

Break the prosciutto into small pieces, fry them in oil in the frying pan. Remove and set aside.

Use the oil from the prosciutto to wilt the spinach. Set aside and repeat the process with the leeks, adding a little oil if necessary. The leeks will take only a few minutes to fry. Use as a garnish as shown in the image.

Ladle the soup into bowls, garnish with wilted seasoned spinach and a piece of prosciutto.

Serve as a starter or as a lunch.

“I wanted a really tasty soup for Anastasia that had no milk in it and was packed full of vegetables. Using potatoes as the thickener, my soups are very hearty and extremely flavourful.”

Brown sugar roasted chicken legs

PREP

Serves a family of 4-6
Prep time: 3-5 minutes
Cooking time: Approx. 35-45 minutes

INGREDIENTS

fresh chicken legs	6-8 washed
soya sauce	2 tbsp
dark brown sugar	1 cup
apple juice	½ cup
sunflower oil	drizzle
sea salt	to taste

TOOLS

1 or 2 large cast Iron frying pans

TIPS

Cast iron pans cook up all foods very well. The taste is unique and well worth the investment. It also holds the heat well after cooking and so you can count on it to keep the food warm too.

Château des Charmes Estate Bottled Aligoté,
VQA Niagara-on-the-Lake

Aligote
Auxelrois
Viewpointe Winery, Lake Erie North Shore

Preheat oven to 425˚F.

Wash the chicken legs and prepare them right in the pan, no extra dishes!

Coat the chicken legs with soya sauce. Drizzle with sunflower oil and sprinkle with dark brown sugar and sea salt.

Add just enough the apple juice into the pan, to almost cover the legs.

Bake uncovered on the bottom rack for 35-45 minutes. Add hot water into the pans when needed while cooking. It may take the full 45 minutes to cook until golden brown.

Perfect little legs, just big enough for the kids to enjoy!

Serve with potatoes, rice or fresh vegetables! So easy!

“Everyone loves chicken legs. Chicken baked this way is simple and irresistible. For the cook, it is soooo easy, and for those who eat them, simply delicious!”

Dill and garlic chickpea hummus for meat and vegetables

PREP

Serves a family of 4-6
Prep time: 15 minutes

INGREDIENTS

chickpeas	1 can drained
garlic cloves	2 chopped
sunflower oil	½ cup
white vinegar	¼ cup
lemon	½
fresh dill	½ cup
garlic powder	2 tsp
sea salt	to taste
fresh ground pepper	to taste

TOOLS

1 bowl
hand-held blender

TIPS

Toss in some toasted sunflower seeds or walnuts. This will enhance the texture completely. This dip is perfect dip for meats, veggies, and fish. Tastes great on French stick too.

Drain the can of chickpeas and rinse under cool water.

Finely chop the garlic cloves and dill.

Put all your ingredients in a bowl, except for the dill. Squeeze in the juice from the lemon.

Blend with hand blender and taste as you go until desired consistency. The texture should be creamy with no bits of chickpeas left.

Add your finely chopped dill and stir it in.

This recipe is designed to be simple and fresh with tastes that are addictive!

Image is shown with baked eggplant sauce on the right side of the glass.

SEE BAKED EGGPLANT RECIPE ON PAGE 308

www.freshalicious.ca

Fresh broccoli from my garden

PREP

Serves a family of 4-6
Prep time: 10 minutes
Cooking time: Approx. 3-4 minutes

INGREDIENTS

broccoli	1-2 heads
sunflower oil	drizzle
sea salt	to taste

TOOLS

1 pot
1 colander

TIPS

Try preparing all your vegetables in simple ways and use their various colours to make dishes more interesting—simple, fast and completely tasty!

Wash the broccoli heads thoroughly in salty water. Cut into pieces and inspect them for any garden friends! They do not make it a point to be seen, so look carefully.

Boil a pot of salted water and blanch the broccoli until it turns a nice dark green. It only takes a few minutes when fresh from the garden.

Drain, place in a serving dish, drizzle with oil and sprinkle with sea salt. That's it!

May I say fresh? Yes!

The broccoli we grew is always sweet,tender and the most beautiful green I ever see. Even if they go into bloom, the flowers are actually quite pretty, and are completely edible.

My kids love broccoli and notice the difference in the home grown taste, texture and colour!

"Freshalicious is all about my love for fresh, delicious foods that are totally healthy! If you choose to be in love with fresh food too, try growing broccoli, it is completely different than what we buy in the grocery stores today."

Summer bean salad with garlic and fresh herbs

PREP

Serves a family of 4-6
Prep time: Approx. 5-10 minutes
Cooking time: none

INGREDIENTS

red kidney beans	1 can 540ml
black beans	1 can 540ml
chick peas	1 can 540ml
spring onions and/or chives	2-4 chopped
white onion	1 small chopped
garlic	1 clove chopped
sunflower oil	¼ cup
fresh lemon	½-1 squeezed
garlic powder	sprinkled to taste
sea salt	to taste

TOOLS

1 serving bowl
1 colander

TIPS

You may want to slice up some fresh tomatoes and cucumbers for this salad. It also handles balsamic vinegar quite well, but fresh lemons are still my favourite! Some of the best salads are made with natural oil and lemons; simplicity replaces high calorie commercial sauces!

Rinse the beans and chickpeas, kidney beans and black beans under cold water unitil the water runs clear and put them directly into the serving bowl you will be using.

Chop up the onions, chives and garlic into small pieces and add them in.

Season first by sprinkling directly on the beans, squeeze the lemon over the seasoning and then pour on the oil.

Toss gently, check the flavour and seaon more if necessary and enjoy!

This bean salad is fun for the kids,fantastic after-work snack that is high in protein and absolutely tasty.

Will stay in the fridge for up to a week, and taste just as good or better as the week passes.

“ A salad like this is quick and simple. It literally takes minutes to prepare and can be eaten as a nice light snack after work or at your next BBQ. ”

Juicy-licious sirloin and pork burgers on whole wheat garlic biscuits

PREP

Serves a family of 4-6
Prep time: 5-10 minutes
Cooking time: Approx. 10 minutes

INGREDIENTS

ground sirloin fresh	1lb
ground pork fresh	1lb
white onion	½ chopped
garlic cloves	3 chopped
oregano fresh	¼ cup chopped
thyme fresh	¼cup chopped
sage fresh or ground	½ tsp
sea salt and pepper	½ tsp
sunflower oil	¼ cup
beer or apple juice	½ cup
crushed crackers	¾ bag Saltines®
eggs	2

GARNISHES

baby spanish onions	10 sliced
roasted red peppers	1 sliced and fried
arugula	1 cup

Optional: ½ cup of sliced kalamata olives for that extra zing! —mixed into the meat

TOOLS

1 mixing bowl
1 tray for finished burgers
1 hand-held blender
1 frying pan for peppers

TIPS

Before making your burgers, try my recipe for Whole wheat burger sized biscuits. They are superb with hamburgers. Try adding olives, or finely chopped sun dried tomatoes to the meat.

BBQ heat 375° - 400° F.

Mix your sirloin and pork in a bowl gently; overmixing will take away from the tenderness in the meat. Add your grated onions, (olives-optional) and spices.

Drizzle on some sunflower oil and add the beer (or wine or apple juice in its place), along with the eggs and crushed crackers.

Mix thoroughly and pat into large balls, flattening them to about 1 inch thick.

Start with a high heat to sear for a quick minute or two, then turn the BBQ down to medium heat and cook to your personal liking.

This keeps the burgers juicy and moist!

While the meat is cooking fry your peppers, season and then blend to create a creamy texture. Add some sunflower oil while blending.

Plate as shown.

Grill some vegetables alongside and you have the perfect Saturday summer lunch BBQ with family and friends.

SEE NEXT PAGE FOR WHOLE WHEAT BURGER-SIZED BISCUITS

"You will need one BBQ and a bunch of hungry, happy friends and a lot of cold beer. Kids love summer barbecues, so spark one up and have fun!"

Whole wheat burger-sized biscuits with thyme and chives

PREP

Makes 26 small or 12 large
Prep time: 5 minutes
Cooking time: Approx. 20-25 minutes

INGREDIENTS

whole wheat flour	2 cups
all-purpose flour	2 cups
baking powder	8 tsp
baking soda	2 tsp
sea salt	1-2 tsp
non-hydrogenated shortening	1 cup
soya milk/almond milk	2 cups
egg	1 for wash
thyme	2 sprigs
small bunch of chives	¼ cup chopped
black pepper	½ tsp

TOOLS

1 bowl
2 cookie trays
2" round cookie cutter for small biscuits
4-6" round cookie cutter for large biscuits

TIPS

Two things about biscuits:if you let the dough rise on the counter before cutting them (3-5 minutes), you will get taller biscuits. Freezing the shortening gives you a flakier lighter texture.

Preheat oven to 425°F.

Freeze the shortening 1 hour before making the biscuits.

Mix all your dry ingredients in a large bowl.

Grate the frozen shortening into the dry mixture and mix with fork just enough so the shortening still stays cold. Pour in the soya or almond milk along with the chives, thyme and seasonings.

The dough will be sticky, so turn out onto a floured surface (kitchen counter will do) and press out with your hands. 1 inch will be good for the small biscuits and minimum 2 inches for the large biscuits.

Using the cookie cutter, cut them out and lay them on the trays roughly 6 per tray, the larger ones may require more space. Beat the egg and brush it on the biscuits.

Bake for about 20 minutes on the middle rack, until they are golden.

Remove and set on a wire rack to cool or serve up right away when making burgers!

“I think all homemade burgers deserve a tastier, more complete bun, full of texture and flavour. Think of this as the Cadillac of buns! ”

Pingue proscuitto pizza with balsamic arugula

PREP

Serves 4-6
Prep time: 10 minutes
Cooking time: Approx. 20-25 minutes

INGREDIENTS

whole wheat pizza dough	1 fresh
SAUCE	
tomatoes	6 large; grated
fresh thyme	3 sprigs
dried oregano, pepper and sea salt	to taste
brown sugar	2-4 tbsp
BALSAMIC DRIZZLE AND ARUGULA	
Balsamic drizzle and arugula	4 tbsp
balsamic vinegar	12 tbsp
sunflower oil	½ tsp
sea salt	to taste
arugula	2 cups
PIZZA	
Kalamata olives	¼ cup
oyster mushrooms	3-4
Spanish onion	1 sliced
garlic cloves	6 chopped
orange pepper	1 sliced
sunflower oil	for frying
prosciutto	300-400 grams
fresh basil	handful

TOOLS

1 pot
hand held blender
3 frying pans
large vented pizza pan or square baking tray

TIPS

Prepare your chopped and sliced pizza ingredients the night before so when you come home, your pizza is assembled in minutes and into the oven.

Preheat oven to 425° F.

Cut up the tomatoes, toss into a pot with the thyme, oregano, sea salt, pepper and brown sugar. Bring to a gentle boil for about 5 minutes; then blend. Test the flavour; add seasonings if needed.

While the sauce is simmering, prepare the arugula and drizzle.

Combine vinegar, sunflower oil, garlic powder, and sea salt to taste. Rinse the arugula and coat with ¼ to ½ of the balsamic drizzle. Set the rest aside for dipping. Coating the arugula prevents shrinking and keeps it moist, and great tasting!

Slice and pit the olives, slice the mushrooms, set both aside. Chop up the onion, garlic, and orange pepper.

Fry the onion and garlic in sunflower oil, season with sea salt, and set aside. Repeat the cooking process for the chopped pepper for about 5 minutes. Set aside.

Repeat the process for the oyster mushrooms for a few minutes on high heat to brown. Set aside.

Roll out the dough, lay it on the pan and pour on your fresh sauce. Lay on the arugula, then the onions & garlic, peppers, mushrooms, olives and finally the prosciutto.

Bake on bottom rack for about 20 minutes, or until it is cooked. Fresh basil (chopped or torn) is for sprinkling on pizza when done.

SEE PAGE 206 FOR PIZZA DOUGH RECIPE

Château des Charmes Estate Bottled Pinot Noir, VQA Niagara-on-the-Lake

Pinot Noir Sangiovese, Valpolicella
Le Chiantigiane Chianti Govornato-uscany Italy, Reuben Valpolicella- Veneto Italy

“Prosciutto is a healthy choice when buying from a local supplier who only uses organic, free-range pork and natural sea salt for curing. Far healthier than commercial proscuitto cured with nitrates.”

Fresh whole wheat pizza dough

PREP

Makes 4 balls
Prep time: 10 minutes
Rising time: 1 hour for dough to rise

INGREDIENTS

whole wheat flour	3 cups
all-purpose flour	4½ cups
extra flour for blending	½ cup
warm water	3 cups
brown sugar	4 tbsp
active dry yeast	4 tbsp
sunflower oil	8-10 tbsp

TOOLS

1 mixer
2 bowls
2 cookie trays for rising dough
(or 6 medium bowls)
pastry brush for oil
plastic wrap to cover the rising dough

TIPS

Different texture and thickness may occur depending on how you make it. If you add salt to your recipe you will slow or stop the dough from rising which will create a thin crust. If you like a bread like crust take the dough out of the fridge, allow it to get to room temperature. Set on oil sprayed pizza tray, and spread dough by hand, cover with plastic wrap and let rise for about one hour. Then add your ingredients and bake for approximately 20 minutes. Enjoy!

Start by measuring your dry ingredients directly into the mixing bowl. Into another bowl, measure the warm water and add the sugar, yeast and oil into it.

Set aside to start the activation process. It may take 5 minutes or so for it to be ready - bubbly and creamy in appearance.

Turn the mixer on low and gradually pour the wet mixture into the dry, blending until the dry flour disappears. The dough should form into a ball with smooth sides around the paddle. If you feel it is too wet, slowly add the extra flour a little at a time until the ball forms. It should be soft and smooth in appearance.

Turn the ball of dough out onto a floured cutting board and cut it into 6 pieces. Knead one at a time for 3-5 minutes by hand, turning the dough into itself, and adding some extra flour if necessary, to make the ball smooth and bouncy.

Set each ball aside on oiled cookie trays until all 6 are formed. Brush them with oil, cover with plastic wrap, and set in a warm area to rise for about 1 hour. Knead each one by hand again for 3-5 minutes.

At this point you can use the dough right away to make pizza or wrap individually or freeze them for use over the next few weeks.

When using from frozen, thaw completely and allow it to rise for an hour at room temperature before making into pizza.

Pizza dough like this is very silky and smooth, and not as springy as commercially made pizza dough. When rolling it out, make sure you roll it to the size of the pizza tray you are using, as it will not shrink. This is for thin crust pizzas, see the tips section.

"I have tried several ways to make the perfect pizza dough. Using these basic ingredients, you can make a thick or thin crust by adjusting the amount of dough used."

Friendship

taking time to enjoy each other

Fine local wines complement seasonally inspired dishes

We have well over 80 fabulous different wineries in the Niagara Peninsula. How do I choose among them all? I was looking for some history—a place that was well established, family run and went back a few generations—and one that makes wines I enjoy.

I chose to visit Château des Charmes for their wine and wine-growing practices. Founded in 1978, they are a family business that takes the time to make magnificent wines using sustainable practices in their vineyards. Many Canadian businesses were started by immigrants, who chose to settle in the Niagara Peninsula. Paul Bosc brought his passion and wine-making know-how from France when he immigrated to Canada in the 1960s. His roots go back to Alsace. Paul is known for his rich heritage of meticulous care in his vineyards, blended together with the art and science of crafting world-class wines. In speaking with Michèle Bosc I discovered that even at 70 years of age, Paul still personally leads the production team and continues to conduct pioneering research.

I was very impressed with the vines; how neatly they are kept even though they have 280 acres to tend. Paul has always believed that in order to make world-class wines you must start with the best grapes. For him this means doing it right, under his own watchful eye. Many of the wines made today come from vines that are more than 25 years old. Care for the environment has always been a priority. When the Château was opened in 1994 it showcased a geothermal cellar to house their French oak barrels. The vines are never irrigated nor are herbicides ever used. The Bosc family believes they are custodians of the land and would rather work with nature to craft such wonderful wines.

Château des Charmes has received of a long list of awards over the years. This fine winery was well worth visiting.

I thoroughly enjoyed taking a tour of their facility. If you're looking to visit a beautiful winery that holds tours daily, educational tastings, weddings and romantic picnics for two, I would definitely recommend the trip.

Château des Charmes' wines are available across Canada and selected cities in the US and around the world.

Pairing your favourite local wine with seasonal food is another way to experience the many layers of wonderful aromas, flavours and complexity that Niagara's world-class wines offer.

Paul Bosc brought his passion and winemaking know-how from France

Wine

Sooo sexy sangria with fresh strawberries and wild strawberry liqueur

PREP

Serves a group of 12
Makes approximately: 7-8 litres

INGREDIENTS

Disaronno®	1 bottle
dark rum	1 bottle
cherry juice	1½ litres
cranberry juice	1½ litres
dry red wine	2 bottles
strawberries	1-2 pints
fresh or frozen local blueberries	1 cup
dried cranberries (optional)	1 handful
gingerale	4-6 cans
Fragoli Liqueur	½ bottle

TOOLS

1 large punch bowl
1 ladle

TIPS

Sangria can be prepared the night before or early in the day. If you soak the berries overnight in the already made sangria, less the ginger ale, they will be potent and heavy with the alcohol. Plus they look less attractive and certainly not fresh. I prefer to wash the fruit and prepare are the final drink just before my guests arrive so they will see a fresh, inviting presentation.

Sooo simple!

Pour all liquids except the gingerale into the large bowl.

Wash the fruit and cut up the strawberries.

Add the fruit and the gingerale just before the guests arrive, this will keep it bubbly and fizzy.

When using frozen fruit, add it as late as possible. This will ensure a fresh look that is very appealing.

www.freshalicious.ca

Wine notes by Hugh Sutherland

Wine is a very personal matter and based on my experience and personal taste, my wine selections in this book are what I consider to be the best selections. However, your own selections are equally important if they please your personal palate. These are suggestions only–not rules.

My early training as a Geological and Environmental engineer have been invaluable in my becoming aware of the value of terroir, climate, and geology in wine growing. This has enabled me to select great wines at good wine prices over the last 40 years.

In today's environment it is very important to remember that wine growing regions have been doing just that for centuries. Because they were best suited to the area—long before Cabernet Sauvignon, Merlot and Chardonnay were hot topics—other varietals were grown in these local regions. Sadly, many growers chose to plant Cab, Merlot & Chard in unsuited regions–resulting in poor wine. Look for Historic varieties in any area—you will be pleased.

Wine roots in poor soil conditions can go up to 400 feet deep to find bedrock and seek flavours. Shallow rootstock (in fertile areas) pick up surface contaminants–so look for wines from poor soil regions.

Due to the fact that not all labels are available everywhere I have chosen to select a Varietal or blend suited to the food with a preferential producer but if the suggested label is not available in your area, ask the store staff to give you a good Estate wine from that region using the same variety. The producers I have suggested are ones I know are good.

The selections are based on how the characteristics of that wine match the flavours of the main ingredients but are modified by any spicing added.

In closing, allow me to offer a few tips for your personal buying & tasting:

- I avoid commercial products. Since their wine must taste the same always, many producers add chemical preservatives and flavours. Nature does not produce the same taste every time.
- Do not try to match wine with a salad that uses vinegar.
- Try chewing the wine. If you don't, you miss some of the five flavour sensors in your mouth.
- Only fill a glass 1/3 full–the nose is as important as the mouth in tasting.

Enjoy!

Hugh Sutherland, CEO *Carriage Trade Wines & Spirits*
Wine Consultant to *Grand Cru Wine & Spirit Merchants (organic)*,
The Upstairs Cellar, *Wine & Leisure.com*

Michèle Bosc, *Château des Charmes*, Niagara-on-the-Lake, also provides wine pairings for her wines.

“Understanding what makes great tasting wines, will help you discover the wine that suits you when sourcing local.”

Fasolakia (potatoes and fresh beans with tomatoes)

PREP

Serves a family of 4-6
Prep time: 10 minutes
Cooking time: Approx. 30 minutes

INGREDIENTS

cooking onion	1 large sliced
white or yellow potatoes	6-8 peeled
fresh beans flat, yellow or green	2 cups cleaned
red tomatoes	4 large grated
tomato paste	½ cup
water	1 cup
cup of chicken stock	1 cup
sunflower oil	¼ to ½ cup
sea salt and pepper	to taste

TOOLS

1 pot

TIPS

Use any kind of fresh bean that is in season or available—yellow, green, flat, or string. Even if the potatoes are overcooked, this dish still tastes great!

First, peel the potatoes and pinch the ends off the beans. Cut the beans in half and quarter the potatoes so they look like pear slices.

Fry the chopped onions just slightly, until they are transparent.

Add the potatoes and fry them with the onions for 3-4 minutes.

Then add the beans and continue to fry for about 5 minutes.

Next, add the grated tomatoes, spices and tomato paste. Grate the fresh red tomatoes over the potatoes and beans.

Carefully cover everything with water, not too much water or your sauce will not form. Add the sunflower oil.

Simmer for about 30 minutes, or until the potatoes are tender and a sauce thickens.

DO NOT COVER—this must reduce while cooking to make a nice tomato sauce.

This dish is a dipper, make sure you have lots of fresh whole grain bread for dipping, one of our personal favourites once the local beans appear.

“Creating simple healthy dishes all in one pot is definitely one of my favourite ways to cook. This is for anyone who loves to cook but wants to maintain their social life by only spending short stints in the kitchen!”

Eggplant cutlet with avocado sauce on a garlic toasted baguette

PREP

Serves a family of 4-6
Prep time: 10 minutes
Cooking time: Approx. 20 minutes

INGREDIENTS

avocado	1
portabella mushrooms	3-4
purple eggplant	1 large
all-purpose flour	¼ cup
whole wheat flour	¼ cup
eggs	3 eggs
whole wheat crackers	2 bags saltines
chicken soup base	2 tbsp
garlic powder	2 tsp
dried oregano	1-2 tsp
fresh thyme	1-2 sprigs
sea salt and pepper	to taste
artisan baguettes	1-2
sunflower oil	for frying
garlic	3-4 cloves
fresh arugula or lettuce	1-2 cups
large green olives optional	¼ cup

TOOLS

4 shallow bowls
2 no-stick frying pans
1 cookie sheet
1 hand held blender

TIPS

So why not try coating fresh, in-season carrots, or parsnips. Try roasting some garlic cloves to add that extra sweetnees to any fresh baguette. And always fry with fresh oil in between fries, to ensure a clean crisp taste.

AVOCADO SAUCE

Clean, pit and chop up the avocado in a bowl. Drizzle it with sunflower oil. Add 1 clove of finely chopped garlic and season with salt as you blend it into a sauce.

MUSHROOMS

Fry the mushrooms in sunflower oil on high heat until they turn brown. Set aside.

CUTLETS

Put the flour in a bowl for coating.

Beat 3 eggs in another bowl for the wash. Mix the finely crushed crackers and seasonings in a third bowl for the coating.

Slice the whole eggplant horizontally into round pieces, 1/ 4 inch thin like round disks. Coat them one at a time, first with flour, then the egg wash, and then the cracker coating. Coat them all and set them on a plate ready for frying.

Fry them in sunflower oil on medium to high heat until golden brown and crunchy. Set them on a drying rack or paper towel until they are all cooked.

If the oil gets dirty, discard it, wipe the pan, and add fresh oil so the crumbs do not burn and affect the taste of the eggplant. Continue coating and frying the rest until they are all done.

Spread sunflower oil on the pieces of baguette and sprinkle with chopped garlic. Place them on a cookie sheet and under the broiler to toast.

Lay your eggplant cutlet on the toasted bread and garnish with lettuce avocado sauce and fried mushrooms. Enjoy!

"Not all sandwiches are created equal. Try using fresh in-season local vegetables with homemade sauces. Eating whatever is in season gives you a variety of new fresh ideas all year long."

BBQ orange cranberry duck sausage

PREP

Serves a family of 4-6
Prep time: 10 minutes
Cook time: Approx. 10-15 minutes

INGREDIENTS

cranberry orange duck sausages	6 fresh
fresh baguettes	2
fresh three herb pesto	2-4 chopped
arugula	2-4 cups

TOOLS

1 BBQ
1 plate for uncooked sausages
1 plate for cooked sausages

TIPS

Gourmet sausages like this need a more attention at the Q, as they are packed full of moisture and sometimes some brown sugar. They will create a bit more smoke and drip making the surface of the grill a little sticky. But it is all good and tasty.

Preheat BBQ to 400°F.

Start by having your pesto prepared along with your arugula and your bread.

How easy is this? Preheat your Q, put your sausages on the grill and after a few minutes flip.Keep grilling until cooked to perfection!

Serve these with my warm potato salad, and some cold beverages.

SEE PAGE 162 FOR PESTO RECIPE

"I like creating simple recipes for guys so they can spice up the flame between themselves and the girls by barbecuing a tasty leaner sausage with a tasty twist!"

Basil chicken and orzo with carrots and celery

PREP

Serves a family of 4-6
Prep time: 10 minutes
Cooking time: Approx. 25-30 minutes

INGREDIENTS

chicken breasts	3 large sliced
white soya sauce	for marinate
celery sticks	2-3 chopped
carrots	2 large
fresh plum tomatoes	4-6 chopped
garlic cloves	2 chopped
white onion	1 large sliced
garlic powder	sprinkled
sea salt and pepper	to taste
water	4 cups
dry orzo	4-6 handfuls
bay leaves	dry whole
fresh basil	¼ bunch
sunflower oil	for frying
sunflower oil	¼cup

TOOLS

1 large stock pot or deep frying pan

TIPS

When making the sauce and pasta together, try starting out with less water — as you go until you get the right consistency. If you're on a tight budget, replace plum tomatoes with a half can of tomato paste; tastes just as great.

Chop and sauté the onion until it is clear, add the garlic and fry for a few minutes in sunflower oil.

Slice and add the chicken (½-1" thick) and sprinkle them with garlic powder.

Fry the chicken on medium in sunflower oil until they turn white, roughly 7 minutes. Remove the chicken slices and set them aside.

Add your chopped vegetables and tomatoes to the onions and garlic. Season them with sea salt and pepper.

Add approximately 4 cups of water, and bring to a boil. Add your orzo and bay leaves and simmer on medium heat until cooked. About 20 minutes.

Just before the orzo is cooked add your chicken and extra sunflower oil and *voila!*

Take note, the extra sunflower oil is optional.

Ready to serve, the sauce should be clear and saucy, and taste really great.Add your fresh basil just before serving!

“This dish is fresh and simple. Cooked all in one pot, it is quick and easy and makes for a great lunch the next day.”

Growing gardens come in many shapes and sizes

If you can find the time in your busy life, why not plant a garden this year? It can be as tiny as a few pots or a 30-by-30-foot space to grow the freshest vegetables around!.

My first garden was approximately 300 square feet and I initially purchased my vegetable seedlings from a local garden centre. Centres usually sell tiny plants, already sprouted, for you to take home and plant in your garden. Water them daily, use soapy water to prevent bugs, and watch them grow.

You can plant asparagus, artichokes, beets, broccoli, brussel sprouts, green beans, pole beans, bush beans, carrots, cauliflower, celery, cucumbers, dandelion, eggplant, garlic, kale, leeks, lettuce, okra, onions, parsnips, peas, hot peppers, sweet peppers, potatoes, pumpkins, spinach, squash, Swiss chard, cherry tomatoes, tomatoes and zucchini. Most fresh herbs such as basil, chives, mint, oregano and parsley are easy to cultivate.

If you lead a busy life and want less work, only plant a few of your favourites. My personal favourites include tomatoes, lettuce, onions, and peppers because of their full flavour when freshly picked. Swiss chard and dandelion also have great taste plus longevity in the garden. You can harvest those two as well as the fresh herbs right up until the snow falls.

My kids really learn a lot by helping me in the garden, whether they plant the seeds or pull the weeds. They wear rubber boots and get totally dirty, which they love! You cannot get the hose out of their tiny little hands if you put them in charge of watering. When the vegetables are ready to pick, they go crazy trying to be the one to pick the most or the biggest! Overall, having a garden at home is truly rewarding. The convenience of walking out into your own backyard to pick fresh tomatoes for a salad or fresh zucchini for the barbecue is totally worth the little bit of work involved. Nicoletta often refers to the garden as our "grocery store!"

> Grow some of the finest produce available, right in your own backyard!

Let's not forget the superb freshness of home-grown veggies plus the low cost—you can't beat that. Novice gardeners may spend the first few years learning how to properly care for the plants, but that leads to a true appreciation for the food we eat. Just think how much work it must take for large farms to get the same foods to us safely and undamaged, while still looking and tasting great. It is well worth the time to plant a garden and grow some of the finest produce available, right in your own backyard!

Green
backyard grocery store

Educational centres excite and motivate kids!

In your local community be motivated to get out and experience educational farming centres and pick-your-own farms. They are a great place to visit for all the family.

Search for them, chat with fiends and neighbours. It's easy to access them or even join. There are many pick-your-own farms to visit on a weekend and pick your own fruits and vegetables right from the fields. This is a great way to spend time with your family, enjoying the outdoors and getting more involved with fresh food.

Most farmers I visited were very concerned about the younger generation not knowing where and how their foods are actually produced. So why not take advantage of what they have to offer?

EDUCATIONAL CENTRES

Gardening at these centres puts you in touch with the natural state of produce. All things grown naturally come in different shapes and sizes—this is not what we are accustomed to. We tend to look at the food for its outward perfection and not necessarily for its inner goodness.

What may save our kids from having a false sense of reality about food are the local learning centres. They grow food, raise animals and have facilities to teach children in outdoor classroom environments about the real food world. I am not sure that every community has this available, but they all should. The kids can get dirty, pick their own fruits and vegetables and learn about food and where it comes from before it gets selected and cleaned up for the grocery store. They learn that carrots can grow crooked, and vegetables can be grown in all shapes and sizes. The sights, sounds and smells are really healthy!

PICK-YOUR-OWN FARMS

Many local communities have pick-your-own farms. The farmers allow you to walk their farm and select exactly what you want, and typically you pay a really great price. My kids really love to take advantage of this and typically over-pick due to their great level of enthusiasm. They learn to follow the avalailability of seasonal foods and always remember when the time is right to get out and go picking!

This is a great environment for the young and old to get out, get exercised and enjoy the fresh air. These are easy, simply fantastic weekend events that the whole family will look forward to enjoying. Everything there revolves around the food we eat.

Getting dirty is just the beginning!

Most farmers I visited were very concerned about the younger generation not knowing where and how their foods are actually produced.

Fresh...
is just the begining

Fresh-from-my-garden salad with carmelized pistachios

PREP

Serves a family of 4-6
Prep time: 10 minutes
Cooking time: Approx. 3-4 minutes

INGREDIENTS

leafy red lettuce	1 bunch
oak lettuce	1 bunch
romaine lettuce	½ bunch
arugula	couple handfuls
baby cucumbers	4-5 sliced
garlic cloves	2-4 chopped
fresh oregano fresh	2 sprigs
lemon thyme fresh	1 sprigs
purple chive flowers if in season	2 fresh

DRESSING

sunflower oil drizzle	½ cup
balsamic vinegar drizzle	¼ cup
garlic powder	½ tsp
garlic	1 clove
sea salt	pinch
lemon juice	couple squeezes
pistachios	1 cup
Amaretto	¼ cup

TOOLS

1 large salad bowl
1 frying pan for pistachios

TIPS

Growing your own lettuce is extremely easy and definitely the tastiest way to in your greens.
When growing your own lettuce it is best to pick early in the morning, or after sunset. Otherwise the lettuce will taste bitter.

This lettuce was grown in my garden—nothing fresher and easier to prepare!

Pick and clean the lettuce leaves, soak in cold water and sea salt for 5 minutes. Rinse them well and lay them out to dry.

Tear your lettuce leaves apart by hand and put them into your salad bowl. Slice the baby cucumbers and toss them in. Add fresh herbs for that really great taste.

To make a perfect dressing I always pour the ingredients right on the salad and toss.

Start by sprinkling the garlic powder, followed by the salt, and then drizzle the balsamic, followed by the oil. Mix, taste and re-season accordingly. The taste is what you make it.

CARMELIZED PISTACHIOS
Carmelizing any nut is easy, Heat up your frying pan, toss in the nuts to toast and get warm.

Throw in a splash or two of Amaretto or your favourite liquor and reduce. You will always get a flame of some sort so turn off your fire before adding your liqueur and resume slowly to cook off the alcohol.

You can toss in any in-season dried fruit to give that sweetness to offset the salty!

Toss in your caramelized pistachios just before serving—*freshalicious*™!

"Adding nuts to your salads gives a crunchy, sweet, salty taste that goes well with a balsamic, garlic and sunflower oil dressing!"

www.freshalicious.ca

Fresh sweet pea, tomato and pepper skewers

PREP

Serves a family of 4-6
Prep time: 5-10 minutes
Cooking Time: Approx. 10 minutes

INGREDIENTS

red cherry tomatoes	1 vine (14)
orange cherry tomatoes	1 vine (14)
sweet peas	12-20
yellow bell peppers	1 cubed
red bell peppers	1 cubed
orange bell peppers	1 cubed

BBQ MARINADE

sunflower oil	¼ cup
fresh lemon	1 fresh
garlic powder	2-3 tsp
sea salt	to taste
herbs- lemon oregano, thyme and basil	up to you!

TOOLS

1 BBQ
1 bag of skewers soaked overnight
1 plate for skewers

TIPS

If you want a sweet crunchy coating, try using maple syrup and drizzle on the skewers when they are almost done. This makes them sticky sweet!

Simply rinse, clean and chop! Slide the fresh colourful veggies onto the skewers, alternating them: tomato, pepper, sweet peas.

You can prepare these a few hours ahead, to be ready for when your guests arrive.

Simply roast them on the BBQ on medium, drizzle them with fresh squeezed lemons, balsamic, sunflower oil and some sea salt!

They do not take long to cook. Some of us like them more cooked than others. Having some fresh herbs like fresh thyme, lemon oregano and basil. also kicks up the flavour,

The amounts on this recipe will vary depending on how much you and your guests love fresh vegetables!

“I find that when preparing fresh kabobs I know I can eat as many as I like without the guilt of over-eating.”

Natural and extremely tasty wild vine leaves

Simply beautiful and great tasting wild vine leaves. My local picking time is early July, and depending on the weather it can be two weeks either way.

Anastaia and Nicoletta go wild about the vine leaves when they are in season. There is not a day that passes around this time of year they are not asking to go and pick the vine leaves. They absolutely love the taste of the Dolmathakia that I am able to prepare throughout the year by preserving vine leaves.

This is a fun way to get out with the girls and teach them about edible foods that grow and sustain without care, pesticides or fertilizers. This is a family tradition passed down by my mother-in-law, Anna. This is and has been a Greek tradition that is shared from mother to daughter. These are prepared just like preserving fruits and vegetables but it's really quick and easy to do.

> Dolmathakia is one of my kids' favourite foods

Dolmathakia is one of my kids' favourite foods, and typically we run out of leaves before the next season starts all over again. I hope you try fixing up your own leaves, you will definitely love the taste.

These kinds of activities can promote outdoor fun in the fresh air and great enjoyment for you and the family. Why not try picking and preparing your own vine leaves this season? They are tastey and you will really love the unique taste that wild vines leaves have.

PREPARING THE VINE LEAVES

First you need to find some wild vine leaves. It is really not difficult as they grow everywhere and are easy to pick. When deciding what leaves to pick, I suggest you pick the five newest leaves on the tip of the vine. As you go further up the vine they are older and tougher. Because they are fresh they beat the imported leaves by far, which tend to be leathery. Start by picking as many as you like - you want them to be a little bigger than your hand. When you get them home you will need to get out a large stock pot, sea salt and some white vinegar. Start by boiling your salted water and add a large splash of vinegar.

You will be cutting off the stems, but be careful not to tear the leaf. Wash them in cold salted water both sides. Set aside for boiling. I count 20 at a time and just lay them in the water. They will start to turn a dark pale green in a few minutes, then flip the leaves to make sure they all get blanched. Remove them and set aside to cool.

Roll each set of 20 in plastic wrap — they can be frozen for up to 6 months. Try keeping them in a sealable container to avoid freezer burn.

DOLMA RECIPE ON NEXT PAGE

Vine leaves

Wild about wine leaves

Dolmas/Dolmathakia (stuffed wild vine leaves)

PREP

Makes approximately 30 dolmas
Prep time: 20 minutes
Cooking time: Approx. 1 to 1½ hours

INGREDIENTS

fresh wild vine leaves hand-picked from field or pre-packaged from store	60
ground meat (½ veal, ½ pork)	1-1½ lb
scented rice dry measurement	1-1½ cups
cooking onion	1 large
dill	½ bunch
lemons	2 squeeezed
sunflower oil	¼ cup
salt & pepper	to taste
water	½ cup

TOOLS

1 large deep frying pan for finished dolmas
1 small frying pan for onions and meat
1 bowl for mixing meats
1 plate for cooking

TIPS

July is typically when the wild grape leaves are ready for picking. A smalll secret for the tender leaves is always pick the five new leaves at the tip of the vine. Keep an eye on the weather, if we have a hot humid start the leaves may be ready in June!

Château des Charmes Estate Bottled Riesling,
VQA Niagara-on-the-Lake

CDC Riesling
Selection Rose Cabernet Sauvignon
Valdivieso Vineyard, Chile

Finely chop up and caramelize the onions in the frying pan with sunflower oil. Add the dill and cook for a few more minutes.

While they are cooking, put the ground meat into a bowl and season with the spices. Add ½ cup of water into the raw meat mixture.

Add the rice to the onions & dill and cook for a few more minutes. Add the uncooked rice, onions & dill to the raw meat mixture. Let it cool and mix by hand.

Double up the vine leaves, shiny sides down, using 2 leaves like 1 big leaf.

Spoon approximately 4 tsp of rice & meat mixture onto the leaves. Roll slightly, then fold in the sides and finish rolling nice and tight. The amount depends on the size of the leaves.

Place the dolmas into a large, deep, dry frying pan, nesting them tightly together, so that they have only a little room to expand while cooking.

Drizzle ½ cup of sunflower oil over the dolmas. Squeeze the fresh lemons over the top and add a little salt.

Cover the dolmas completely with water and invert a large plate over them to keep them from coming apart during cooking.

Cook at a gentle boil for approximately 1 hour and 15 minutes. Check them often and add warm water as required until they are cooked.

There should be a little juice left that tastes absolutely amazing when they are done . Open a dolma from the middle of the pan to see if the rice is completely cooked. If so, they are done!

“These tasty little dolmas/dolmathakia are just the right size for the kids. Dolmas are a big favourite in our house and huge on fresh taste!”

Taste the difference of naturally raised pork

Sourcing locally, organically grown meats can be challenging for all of us. Choosing where to start and building a strong relationship with a brand or a well known farmer is the beginning. Once this is established the rest is really quite simple. Pork is a really great tasting meat if grown organically and allowed to live a natural pastured life.

WHOLE CIRCLE FARM

Whole Circle Farm is a family run farm that boasts pastured pork, beef and free-range chickens. The chickens were housed in a old yellow school bus. How fun is that? The pigs and cattle are free to graze and live a stress-free life, and definitely long enough to produce great tasting meats. Whole Circle Farm are known for raising livestock with no antibiotics, no growth promoters, chemicals, or genetically modified organisms. They recieved *The Sustainable Famer Award* last year that was well earned.

Naturally grown, antibiotic-free pork is a healthier, better tasting choice

BERETTA ORAGANIC FARMS

Mike and Cynthia Beretta of Beretta Organic Farms, are committed to providing organic meats for those looking for healthier choices. They claim that the food should be as natural as the soil. They raise pigs, beef, cattle, sheep, turkeys, chickens and laying hens. All organically grown. They are also high quality meat packagers who take pride in packaging organically raised meats and selling specialty grocery store chains.

What makes these farmers different is that they use more traditional ways to raise their animals, naturally with time. No GMO's, chemicals, growth promoters, or antibiotics.

For the most part, when raising pigs commercially, different techniques are used to grow them faster to produce more and create a specific texture and moisture in the meat. This type of farming changes the meat and we loose touch with what the real taste should be like.

On average, it only takes four months to raise a pig commercially, in a confined space with hundreds of other pigs, before it goes to slaughter.

Free-range or certified co-op pigs, however, are raised to mature in 6-12 months. They also live stress-free lives, are pastured, eat grass, and get plenty of exercise.

Raising the pigs naturally and organically allows fat to form, enhancing the full flavour of the pork. Both methods are apparently equal in terms of cost. So why not choose the more natural organic meats over commercially grown meats?

The reality is that naturally grown, antibiotic-free pork is a healthier, better tasting choice.

Pork
...this one went to market

IMAGES FROM WHOLE CIRCLE FARM

Seared pork tenderloin on a bed of sweet peas

PREP

Serves a family of 4-6
Prep time: 10 minutes
Cooking time: Approx. 20-25 minutes

INGREDIENTS

organic pork tenderloin	1
local ice wine	1 cup
sweet peas	4-6 cups
sunflower oil	drizzle
sea salt and pepper	to taste

TOOLS

1 large cast iron pan
1 pot for blanching

TIPS

When sweet peas are in season and they are local they are at their best, local and full of flavour. When choosing an ice wine, try new flavours. Why not toss on some fresh berries or finish off the meat with a raspberry or apricot preserve, from the previous season?

Preheat oven to broil.

Start by rinsing the sweet peas. Set aside. Rinse pork and dry on a paper towel. Oil your pan and sear the seasoned meat on all sides to seal in the flavour.

Set under the broiler and stay close by to turn often to avoid burning. You want to place the meat high enough to cook but not close enough to splatter. Keep turning until the meat is cooked through.

When it is done, set aside covered with foil, and use the juices from the meat to create a really great tasting juice to drizzle on the pork before serving.

Reduce the ice wine over high heat until desired reduction occurs. Set aside.

Have a pot of boiling water ready to blanch the peas, about 3-4 minutes, and remove.

Plate as shown in the picture; this dish is meant to be simple and full of flavour.

"Simplicity is in my nature. Often, the more simple the food is, the better it tastes. Serving the meat with just the vegetables not just looks beautiful but is extremely satisfying."

Sticky tenderloin, sweet pea and red pepper rice diamonds

PREP

Makes 20 Appetizers
Prep time: 20 minutes
Cooking time: Approx. 30 minutes for the rice, Approx. 15-20 minutes to fry

INGREDIENTS

STICKY RICE	
scented rice	1 cup
salted water for the rice	2 cups
garlic powder	1-2 tsp
sunflower oil	for frying
TENDERLOIN	
tenderloin	2 sliced very thin
maple syrup	¼ cup
sea salt	to taste
VEGETABLES	
sweet peas	25
arugula	½ cup
red pepper	1 sliced
sunflower oil	for frying

TOOLS

1 large pot for rice
1 large pot for blanching
2 large no-stick frying pans
1 1 inch diamond shaped cookie cutter (sprayed with no-stick oil)
2-3 beautiful serving platters

TIPS

The rice must be sticky in order for the diamonds to retain their shape. It may take a few tries to get the perfect sticky rice. Add water gradually to get the desired texture. If you add too much water right from the beginning, you cannot take it back.

STICKY RICE
Add your rice to cool water, rinse once if you like and bring to a boil. Continue cooking on medium heat, allowing the water to reduce but do not let the rice get dry, and if it does add a little bit of water and continue cooking until the rice splits and is sticky. Set aside to cool.

VEGETABLES
Blanch the peas in salted boiling water for 3-4 minutes, rinse with cool water and set aside.

Slice the red pepper into small pieces, and fry in hot salted sunflower oil. Fry for 3-4 minutes so the pepper retains its colour. Set aside.

Have the arugula rinsed and ready for plating.

RICE DIAMONDS
Start by taking the sticky rice by hand and press into the cookie cutter, pop out on a plate ready for frying.

It is a good idea to make all of these before you start frying them. Heat up the pan to medium, so they will brown not burn. Cook each side 3-4 minutes until golden.

TENDERLOIN
While they are frying heat up the second pan for the tenderloin, fry in sunflower oil for a few minutes, then pour in the maple syrup and turn up the pan to high. Fry until the syrup becomes sticky and set aside.

Cut the rice diamonds in half and assemble them as in the image: the arugula as the base, the bottom of the rice diamond, next the peas, peppers and the top of the rice diamond. Finish it off with the sticky tenderloin and serve.

"Appetizers like these are fun and extremely tasty! You can, however, add a little sticky drizzle, and a few chilies to top them off if you like."

Delicious summer fruits ready for picking

We are very fortunate to have a full range of experienced growers in the Niagara Peninsula who cultivate some of the world's finest fruits. It is amazing that, even with the short growing season, they are able to produce some of the most healthy, tasty, top quality fruits available.

After searching for a very large family owned fruit growing business that had been in operation for a long period of time, I was intrigued by one particular farm that is still very traditional in our modern world.

Located in the Niagara Peninsula, Cherry Avenue Farms, with well over 10,000 fruit producing trees, has been owned and run by the Moyer family since 1799 - that's 211 years! They are a family run farm with a great reputation in their field for producing some of the finest fruits around.

My family and I love to travel to Tom's farm to pick our own cherries, peaches, plums and apricots. They have a wonderful old red tractor that takes you to the fields to pick what your heart desires. It is a joy to watch how much fun the kids have, competing over who is going to fill their baskets first! There are ladders scattered throughout the trees. If you are not afraid to climb up high, the best fruits are ready and waiting to be picked.

Tom and I chatted for a while on one particular visit, and we discussed today's farming practices versus farming years ago. He has had to overcome incredible changes in order to remain competitive and give consumers what we want. He also supplies many large grocery retailers and has had to accommodate their ever-changing requirements. Globalization is not easy!

I know that his fruits make it to our local grocery stores and he has some of the finest fruits I have ever eaten.

> Pick our own cherries, peaches, plums and apricots.

I am certain that you have a farmer just like Tom in your community, who works very long hours all season long ready and willing to supply you with fabulous fresh in-season fruits.

The reality is that if we choose to buy our fruits for price, (when in season), and the fruit comes from overseas, who is going to buy our local producers' fruit? It is fresh for a while but after a short time it will spoil, and he is at a loss. This is a really good reason to buy local and in season.

The next time you're at the grocery store, remember my story, and buy locally grown fruits.

Family
get picking!

Preserving fresh, delicious flavours for the winter months

Since our growing season is a little short, we seem to be hit all at once with so much fresh local produce.

One way to save that wonderful fresh taste, especially with fruit, would be to make jam or preserving the fruit whole. You can also do vegetables and pickles all the same, but there is something special about making your own jam - every time you eat it, it tastes just a good as the day it was picked.

Making jam does not have to be done once a year. As the seasons change and we see local strawberries, take the time to preserve them for when they are in season. It takes very little time. With a bit of prep you can control the taste and actually make it really good for you.

I like to use half the sugar and I prefer cane sugar and real pectin for thickening. When making preserves at home, you can skip the extra sugar that is often found in commercial jams. Jams do not have to be full of sucrose, glucose and fructose, as those sugars are not the sugars we want to be eating.

When making preserves at home, you can skip the extra sugar that is often found in commercial jams.

WHAT YOU WILL NEED FOR MAKING JAMS

ITEMS

Jars, lids and canner (all sterilized)
1 deep stainless steel saucepan
Fruit cleaned (chopped and/or pitted)
Fruit Juice
Lemon Juice
Pectin

FRUIT

4 cups of fruit
1 cup of juice
1 package of Pectin

MAKING THE JAM

3-4 minutes of hard boiling for the fruit. Then you fill your jars almost to the top (stop at the neck). Tighten lids hand. Then boil for 10 minutes!

That's it!

How simple is that? You can mix your favourite fruits together, like yellow plums and peaches, or raspberries and blueberries, even rhubarb and peaches! The possibilities are endless and the results are fantastic.

To process them for good food storage you need to boil them for 10 minutes covering the jars at least one inch. Sometimes it takes up to 24 hours for the jam to set.

Just keep everything clean, be adventurous and mix fruit flavours. Personally I could not go back to commercially made jams once I started this process. Trust me, you will too.

Fresh Jam

packed full of fall flavours

freshalicious™ fruit!

PREP

Serves a family of 4-6
Prep time: 15 minutes

INGREDIENTS

fresh strawberries	2 packages
fresh raspberries	2 packages
fresh blueberries	2 packages
green seedless grapes	1 large bunch
red seedless grapes	1 large bunch
fresh maple syrup	½-1 cup
reduced fruit	1-2 cups

TOOLS

large bowl for salted water
1 or 1 attractive serving plate
and/or single serving dishes

TIPS

Here is how I keep strawberries fresh and ready for up to a week in the fridge. First rinse them in salted cold water as soon as you bring them home, cut off the stems if you wish and place them on a damp paper towel in an air-tight container. Another way is to rinse them the same way, remove most of the water and put them in a glass mason jar and in the fridge.
Lastly with all fruits, try sourcing local, you will get the best tasting, juiciest fruits packed full of nutrition.

Wash all the fruit in a cold water and sea salt bath.

Leave them all whole and the grapes in bunches for a casual occasion.

For a more elegant occasion, cut the grapes into sets of three with scissors, cut the strawberries into quarters, and group them with the rest on a pretty serving dish.

Sometimes we forget that a healthy dessert can just be fresh fruit! This is a great healthy alternative to baked goods.

The prettier you make it look, the more the kids will eat. Choose the tiny fruits, they're easy to pick up and are usually very colourful.

This particular display of fresh fruit was not intended to show all of these fruits in season. I did this to inspire everyone to get busy eating and plating fresh fruit.

Where I live strawberries, grapes, raspberries and blueberries are all in season.

Using maple syrup for dipping fresh fruit is fun and makes it just that much more of a dessert!

Absolutely *freshalicious™*!

"Sourcing fresh local fruits in your area is quite easy, it is really up to us to choose local and support them as a neighbour and a friend."

Anastasia's fresh fruit smoothies

PREP

Serves a family of 4-6
Prep time: Approx. 5 minutes

INGREDIENTS

BLUEBERRY AND RED CURRANT SMOOTHIES

ice cubes	1 cup
apple juice (chilled)	1 cup
blueberries (fresh)	1 package
red currants(fresh)	1 package
bananas	1-2
vanilla soya milk	2 cups

STRAWBERRY RHUBARB SMOOTHIES

ice cubes	1 cup
apple juice chilled	1 cup
strawberries fresh	1 package
rhubarb sweetened/precooked	2 cups
bananas	1-2
vanilla soya milk	2 cups

TOOLS

1 blender
margarita or martini
glasses!

TIPS

When making dairy-free smoothies you can also look for almond milk and rice milk, your local grocery store carries all three.

Keep aside a few berries for the garnish.

Rinse all your fresh fruit first. Toss the fruit into the blender.

Then toss in the ice cubes, and blend. While blending, pour in the soya milk.

Blend until smooth and serve right away!

Making it fun is the best way to get kids to eat fresh fruit without any hassle.

Having the kids help to prepare fruit smoothies makes a huge difference in how exciting fruit can be to them!

“Anastasia wanted me to create a dairy-free smoothie. This one is perfect for her and low cal for those who love cold summer treats!”

Organically grown food; would you support the change?

I thought this was a very valid question to ask all farmers, whether they were fruit or vegetable growers. The fact is that most of us are unclear as to what real organic farming is. The word has been used loosely in marketing and labeling so I thought I would share with you what they said. And in the end you may agree with me.

I made several visits to many farms to shed some light on organic farming and was not surprised at what I heard. Organic farming is possible but there are things to be considered before a farm operation decides to go that way.

One farmer enlightened me with some interesting information that really shed some light on the whole farming world. Farming is not easy and that is no surprise—the elements of nature alone that they have to contend with every year can create highs and lows in production. Sometimes there is not enough rain, or it's too humid, or pests may be an issue. Crops always vary depending on the weather. Mix in global climate change, economic conditions and recessions, mergers and competition and farmers may see a drop in customers. Instead of having a very large number of commercial buyers, farmers now have to deal with only a few very large buyers and distributors.

All these variable are contributing factors leading either to success and sales, or to poor yields and losses.

As a result, the farming/grocery landscape has changed dramatically.

When a farmer decides to go organic, he is exposing his entire farm, stability and future income to uncertainty—a very scary proposition for any farmer. Production is likely to go down for up to three years until they get stabilized.

Organic farming is possible but there are things to be considered

Needless to say, switching to organic growing methods is a big decision, and farmers need to consider it very carefully. Switching is possible, but requires good strategic planning to make the change successful.

Government support can be greatly helpful when an operation decides to switch to being organic, but we all stand to win!

Any day of the week, organically produced food is the best, and it can be done.

I foresee that the only way this can happen on a large scale would be through our support for higher farming standards and choosing to purchase local organic foods. The more we are involved with our food the better quality it will be!

Fruits of love
naturally grown

Summer peach plum shortbread tart

PREP

Serves minimum of 12
Prep time: 5 minutes
Baking time: 1st bake Approx. 30 minutes
2nd bake Approx. 30 minutes

INGREDIENTS

COCONUT - Start by toasting the coconut on an open baking tray at 350° F for 5-7 minutes until it turns a little brown. Set aside to cool.

fancy coconut	1 cup

DOUGH

non-hydrogenated lard	1 cup
brown sugar	1 cup
vanilla	1 tsp
whole wheat flour	3 cups
salt	½ tsp
toasted cocnut	1 cup you prepared

FRUIT RECIPE

large firm local peaches	7-8
large firm red plums	2-3
homemade peach plum jam	2 cups
local honey	½ cup
lavender	for decoration

TOOLS

1 baking tray
2 very large bowls for dough and peach slices
1 bowl for plum slices
mixer
12 inch tart pan with removable bottom
1 large frying pan

TIPS

Making a fresh tart like this gives you the option to cook it as long as you like. Fruit can be eaten a little firm and full of flavour. No glucose, fructose or tons of sugar, just the natural sweetness of really fresh fruit.

Preheat oven to 350° F.

CRUST

Mix the brown sugar and lard and blend until creamy, adding the vanilla. Add the flour, coconut and salt and mix completely, it may look kind of crumbly but this is proper.

Pour the mixture directly into the tart pan. Shape and press it into the sides and bottom, forming a nice crust. Press it tight so it will bake perfectly.

Place in the oven at 350° F and bake for approximately 15 minutes, just to cook through. Remove and set aside.

FRUIT MIXTURE

As seen in the image, the peaches are sliced into small, identical sized pieces.

The same is required for the plums, and set them aside in a separate bowl.

Mix the jam and honey in the frying pan on medium heat and then add the peach slices carefully. Cook down the peaches, maybe halfway, for about 5-7 minutes.

We do not want to lose the integrity of the pieces by turning them to mush, so you will decide how long based on what you see. I prefer the fruit to be a little firm. If you like it softer, cook for another 15 minutes or so.

Once they are done, pour the peach mixture into the tart shell, arrange the plum slices as shown, and toss on some lavender. Bake for about 30 minutes, or until the crust shows some browning and the fruit is cooked to your liking.

Remove and cool on a rack, pop out of the pan, slice and serve.

“This is one of my favourite desserts and it screams summer! Simply freshalicious at its best.”

Caledon cherry pie with candied maple syrup and toasted almonds

PREP

Serves a family of 4-6
Prep time: 20 minutes
Baking time: Approx. 35-40 minutes

INGREDIENTS

phyllo pastry	25 sheets
cherries	6 cups pitted
cranberry juice	1 cup
brown sugar	½ cup
lemon juice	1 tbsp
cornstarch	2 tbsp
sunflower oil	½ cup
almonds	½ cup chopped

SYRUP

canadian maple syrup	1 cup
brown sugar	½ cup

TOOLS

1 pot
1 frying pan for reduction
9 x 13 glass pan

TIPS

You can substitute any fresh, in-season fruit such as red plums with pecans. Try using peaches, or apricots. It really is an all-season recipe!

Preheat oven to 325°F.

This cherry pie is made with phyllo and can be baked with the top open or closed.

Chop and toast the almonds in a hot frying pan until they brown. Set them aside. They may be sprinkled in the pie and/or on top.

Combine the pitted and halved cherries, cranberry juice, lemon juice and brown sugar in a medium sized pot and cook for about eight minutes on medium heat until the cherries are half cooked.

Slowly add the cornstarch, mixed with a little water, and keep stirring until you get a thick and even consistency. Like any pie filling, the cherry sauce should be thick enough to spoon over the crust without dripping.

Lightly oil the bottom of the baking dish.

Fully cover the bottom of the dish with a minimum of 12 phyllo sheets, overlapping and lightly oiling each layer. Sprinkle in some toasted almonds if you wish. Pour the cherry filling over the phyllo layers and spread evenly.

I like to use a good pizza cutter to slice the remaining phyllo into strips that are approximately 2 inches wide for the top of the pie.

Layer them over the cherries, in a criss-cross pattern oiling in between phyllo layers. Add toasted almonds on top if you like.

CONTINUES ON NEXT PAGE

"Simple and easy to make, tasty cherry pie with all the natural sugary sweetness of maple syrup."

Caledon cherry pie with candied maple syrup and toasted almonds cont'd

CONTINUED FROM PREVIOUS PAGE

Bake on the middle rack for 45 minutes or until the top and bottom layers become golden.

About 10 minutes before the pie is cooked, make the maple syrup and brown sugar reduction by boiling it down in a small pot until the sugar dissolves completely.

There are two ways to apply the syrup.

You may drizzle it around the edge of the pie when it is hot to ensure the syrup gets down under the pie, in between phyllo layers.

OR

You may want to drizzle some as above, but save a small amount and reduce it further, more like a thick candy, and drizzle it on top to get the look I created in the picture.

A perfect sweet dish for summer parties when our cherries are in season.

“I chose to combine two recipes to create a new pie. Traditionally baklava is full of syrupy sugar. I gave up the same old tired pie crust, one way to turn up the flavour and texture on this one!”

Whole wheat sugar cookies

PREP

Makes 24 cookies
Prep time: 10 minutes
Baking time: Approx. 5-7 minutes

INGREDIENTS

non-hydrogenated shortening	¾ cup
light brown sugar	¾ cup
egg	1
vanilla	1 tsp
whole wheat flour	1 cup
all-purpose flour	1 cup
baking powder	1 tsp
baking soda	1 tsp
ground cardamom	1 tsp

TOOLS

1 large bowl
2 non-stick baking sheets

TIPS

If you want half of the cookies to be chocolate, once the dry ingredients are completely mixed, take half of the dough, make it into 2 balls, cover and set aside. Add ¼ cup of cocoa to the half remaining in the bowl, mix it in along with 2 tbsp of cranberry juice. This gives you the two types of cookies shown.

Preheat oven to 375°F.

Cream the shortening with the brown sugar until smooth. Add the egg and vanilla and beat until creamy.

Add the dry ingredients and blend until the flour is completely mixed.

Divide into 4 balls and keep the other ones covered with plastic wrap. Roll each ball out and let the kids use your seasonal cookie cutters. They will love it!

Using a spatula, put the cookies on the sheet about 1 inch apart.

Bake for 5-7 minutes, take out and cool completely on a cooling rack.

There are really two ways to make these cookies. If you bake them for 5 minutes, they will be chewy and soft; if you bake them for 7-10 minutes, they will crisp up nicely and have a nice crunchy texture.

A perfect recipe for Christmas, Easter, Hallowe'en, or any time you want them. Decorating is easy, but it's healthier if you make your own sugar icing as opposed to buying it pre-made.

Honestly, if you get your kids involved in making the cookies, and you let them eat them warm from the oven sprinkled with icing sugar, they will probably not ask to coat them with icing and just eat them the way they are. It works for my kids!

“All kids love to decorate and eat cookies when the festive seasons roll in. These pass the test without the icing. A little whole wheat goes a long way without sacrificing great taste.”

Wild blueberry and honey tarts with caramelized walnuts

PREP

Makes 12 large tarts
Prep time: 15-20 minutes
Baking time: Approx. 35-40 minutes

INGREDIENTS

BLUEBERRY FILLING

wild blueberries	3 pints
use frozen berries when not in season	
cinnamon	sprinkle
vanilla	1 tsp
unpasteurized Honey	¼ cup
cherry brandy	¼ cup
cornstarch	2-4 tbsp
sunflower oil for the phyllo	¼ cup
phyllo pastry sheets	12 sheets

WALNUT TOPPING

chopped walnuts	¾ cup
Amaretto®	½ cup

TOOLS

1 large pot
brush and dish for oiling
muffin tin(s)
1 frying pan

TIPS

To make things easy, oil all your sheets, layer them and then cut them with a pizza cutter. You will have these made and in the oven in no time! Lay one phyllo tart at a time, making sure each sheet has been brushed with oil. This makes perfectly crunchy pastry.

Preheat oven to 375°F.

Start by cooking down the fruit with cinnamon, vanilla and honey, for about 10 minutes.

Add the cherry brandy and reduce. Then thicken with cornstarch and cool.

Prepare 3-4 sheets of phyllo, oiling lightly in between each one. Using a pizza cutter cut them into squares, just big enough to fit each muffin tin.

Place them into the muffin tins, one tart at a time. Fill each tart fully with the cooled fruit. Try not to fill them too high or they will bubble all over the place, making a messy presentation; can't have that!

Bake them for about 35-40 minutes, or until the phyllo is golden to brown.

WALNUT TOPPING
Put the chopped walnuts into a hot frying pan and add the amaretto. Cook down until no juice remains and the walnuts are sticky. Set aside to cool while the tarts are baking.

Take the tarts out of the oven when cooked and put 1½ tsp of nuts on each one.

Best when served warm!

“Using locally grown in-season fruits has priority with me. Creating healthy, simple desserts is really easy. Your family can enjoy sweets without eating too much sugar and preservatives!”
www.freshalicious.ca

Crispy, chewy, cranberry coconut cookies

PREP

Makes 36-48 cookies
Prep time: 10 minutes
Chill time: 1 hour
Baking time: Approx. 12-15 minutes

INGREDIENTS

brown sugar	1¾ cups
sunflower oil	½ cup
fresh eggs	2 large
vanilla	1 tsp
all-purpose flour	1 cup
whole wheat flour	¾ cup
baking powder	1 tsp
baking soda	1 tsp
dried cranberries	1¾ cups
shredded coconut	1½ cups

TOOLS

mixer
1 bowl for dry ingredients
2 non-stick cookie trays

TIPS

This cookie recipe is my most versatile recipe yet! You can switch it up with nuts and any kind of dried in-season berry to create in-season cookies. Using oil gives a crunchy texture. Try using non-hydrogenated margarine; this will give you a perfectly chewy soft cookie.

Preheat oven to 335˚F.

Beat the sugar, oil, eggs and vanilla with a mixer until creamy.

In a separate bowl combine the flours, baking powder and baking soda.

Mix dry ingredients slowly into wet ingredients with mixer on low.

Once combined, add cranberries and coconut, again with mixer on low.

Chill for one hour.

Pinch a spoonful or two—it tastes great! Use a teaspoon or tablespoon to portion the dough.

Bake at 335˚F for 12-15 minutes, or until golden.

Let cool completely on a wire rack before putting into glass container.

You can make these with a more local influence by substituting your coconut with oatmeal, any crushed cereal and tossing in some local seeds. Be creative!

“I was challenged to come up with a cookie that is simple, light, chewy and crisp. This one is close to cookie perfection!”

Everyone loves delicious cookies and cakes!

We love our cookies and cakes. What makes a really great tasting cookie? Texture is really what we look for: chewy, soft or crunchy. And what makes a really great cake: the softness, the moistness, and the taste sensations that revolve around the perfect cake.

Really, why do we love our cookies and cakes? They are absolutely delicious and extremely addicting. What makes the best cookie and cake recipes are ones that you can eat all the time without feeling the pressure of gaining weight!

This would mean someone would have to create some really great recipes. You have probably experienced dry cookies—cookies that taste like hay? Or, what about the cookies that seem uncooked? And then there are the ones that have absolutely no taste at all.

The same goes for cakes. It seems that the finest bakers horde all the great recipes and we have little to choose from. There are dry cakes, sandy, tasteless cakes, and finally, flat cakes that refuse to rise.

What is it that I do differently with my cakes and cookies? My cookies are made without butter, milk or cream, contain low amounts of sugar, have no glucose or fructose, have no fillers or preservatives, and definitely no food coloring.

I use whole wheat and all-purpose flours (usually 50/50), nuts, whole grains such as flax and fresh and dried fruits. I replace milk with rice or soya milk, using fruit juices as well. Oh, and I rarely put icing on cakes.

When making my cakes and cookies, I use local in-season ingredients.

We should all eat really great tasting cookies and cakes and my simple secret is to keep it as natural as possible. Why should we stop eating them when we can make them taste great, using healthy ingredients?

The good news is that you purchased this cookbook to try new recipes! In the short-term, if you need to buy cookies and cakes for the little ones and yourself, read the label before you make the purchase. This will give you the opportunity to leave it on the shelf if you're not satisfied with the ingredients. There is nothing wrong with being fussy about the food you are going to consume. Try avoiding white refined flours, hydrogenated fats, glucose, high fructose, dextrose, corn syrup solids, modified ingredients and any funky names you cannot understand. These are all a definite no-no when choosing packaged cookies!

Use my recipes as they are and you will see how much you love my cookies!

Try avoiding white refined flours, hydrogenated fats, glucose, high fructose, dextrose, corn syrup solids, modified ingredients and any funky names you cannot understand.

Cookies

home-made cookies rock!

Excited about fresh fall squash and root vegetables!

Autumn in Canada and the upper United States is a magnificent time of the year that many of us enjoy!

The leaves turn shades of beautiful colours, crimson reds, glowing yellows and the most wonderful bright oranges I have ever seen. Sometimes, from a distance, the leaves take on a pale pink color. The corn has turned brown as have the soya fields, and every few miles you see a stand with a sign that says Corn For Sale! The farmers' markets are buzzing and the local produce is here. It is truly the most bountiful time of the year for fresh fruit and vegetables. And fresh, man is it fresh! The anticipation of eating really great tasting food is everywhere and this is when we all put on our best chef hat and get busy! We have the most fresh produce available at this time of year.

Canning and making sauce is one way of holding onto that fresh taste we can save for the winter months.

So why not get out and enjoy!

september • apples • apricots • peaches • plums • blueberries, cucumbers • sweet corn • green beans • carrots • turnips • beets • peppers • spinach • celery • swiss chard • green onions • zucchini, potatoes • blueberries • celery • red and black currents • garlic • mushrooms • snow peas • peppers • radicchio • rapini • raspberries • strawberries • eggplant • plums • grapes • leeks • musk melon • nectarines • parsnips • snow peas • squash • brussel sprouts • crab apples • spanish onions • zucchini • **october** • broccoli • cabbage • carrots • turnips • onions • beets • peppers • celery • garlic • mushrooms • snow peas • peppers • rapini • radishes • raspberries • sprouts • tomatoes • eggplant • leeks • parsnips • pears • snow Peas • zucchini • **november** • apples • pears • cauliflower • asian vegetables • chinese cabbage • turnips • radishes • onions • potatoes • squash • pumpkins • cranberries • cucumber • garlic • leeks • lettuce • spanish onions • peppers • rutabaga • sweet potatoes • mushrooms • pc

Autumn

young and loving it!

Baked sweet potatoes with maple cranberry reduction

PREP

Serves a family of 4-6
Prep time: 5 minutes
Cooking time: Approx. 45 minutes

INGREDIENTS

sweet potatoes	6 large
apple juice	¼ cup
sunflower oil	drizzle
dark brown sugar	sprinkle
sea salt	to taste

CRANBERRY REDUCTION

frozen or fresh cranberries	1½ cups
Canadian maple syrup	1 cup
cornstarch	1-2 tbsp

TOOLS

1 frying pan
11 x 15 baking pan
foil

TIPS

The less mashing you do to root vegetables the better they taste, and your presentation can be bold and beautiful. Try this with regular potatoes and squash!

Preheat oven to 400°F.

Wash and cut the sweet potatoes in half, leaving the skins on. Score them and place them in the baking pan, skin side down.

Add the apple juice, drizzle with sunflower oil, sprinkle brown sugar and sea salt.

Cover with foil and bake for roughly 45 minutes, or until cooked.

At the end, broil for a few minutes to brown them a little, this creates a tastier sweet potato.

CRANBERRY REDUCTION
Cook the cranberries and maple syrup in a frying pan until the berries start to break. Check the sweetness—you may add sugar or more maple syrup before thickening.

Add the cornstarch (mixed with cold water) pouring in a little at a time stirring until you get your desired thickness.

“Totally local produce, made so simple, yet full of fantastic flavour! This is an easy and impressive way to serve fresh fall vegetables!”

www.freshalicious.ca

Red and white (Canadian) Olympic bean soup

PREP

Serves 4-6
Prep time: 20 minutes
1st Cooking time: Approx. 1 hour
2nd Cooking time: Approx. 1½ - 2 hour

INGREDIENTS

OVERNIGHT SOAK - The night before, soak the beans in 8 cups of salted water.

dried red kidney beans	2 cups
dried white kidney beans	2 cups
water for soaking	8 cups
sea salt	1 tsp

NEXT DAY - Rinse the soaked beans, drain the water and refill with at least 8 cups of fresh water. Boil for about 1½ hours. Drain, rinse and drain again.

chicken stock	4 cups
water for cooking soup	10 cups

SOUP - Fill the large stock pot with the chicken stock and 10 cups of fresh water. Add the beans and resume cooking on high until boiling. Reduce to a steady simmer after adding the vegetables (see below).

large carrots	3 chopped
celery stalks	2 chopped
medium Spanish onions	2 sliced
sprigs	2 sprigs
curry	1½ tsp
smokey paprika	1½ tsp

CONTINUED NEXT PAGE

TOOLS

1 pot for soaking and cooking beans
colander
1 large stock pot
3 prep bowls for veggies
roasting tray
frying pan
bowl for fried steak garnish

Preheat oven to 350°F.

Clean and prepare your vegetables - chop the carrots, de-vein and chop the celery and chop up the onions.

Set aside in bowls until the stock pot starts to boil. Toss the veggies into the boiling chicken stock and beans.

Season with the spices listed and taste as you go, re-season as necessary. Stir in the tomato paste until it dissolves completely.

Reduce the heat to obtain a steady simmer and continue until the beans and vegetables are fully cooked. This may take another 1-1½ hours.

As the soup is simmering, rinse the baby potatoes, cut into quarters, lay them on a baking tray, season well with sea salt, black pepper and garlic powder, drizzle with sunflower oil, cover with foil.

Bake in the oven at 350°F for about ½ hour.

When they are done turn on the broiler, remove the foil and roast them until they turn a little brown, about 3-5 minutes.

Cover again and set aside to add to soup just before serving.

CONTINUED NEXT PAGE

"2010 was one of the best years in Canadian Olympic history! This soup is made with all of them in mind. Great job Canadian Olympians!"

Red and white (Canadian) Olympic bean soup cont'd

PREP

Serves 4-6
Prep time: 20 minutes
1st Cooking time: Approx. 1 hour
2nd Cooking time: Approx. 1½ - 2 hour

INGREDIENTS

CONTINUED FROM PREVIOUS PAGE

ground sage	½ tsp
oregano	½ tsp
sea salt	to taste
fresh ground pepper	to taste
garlic powder	2 tsp
tomato paste	½ can
baby potatoes (for roasting)	12-15 cut into ¼'s
sunflower oil	drizzle
sirloin steak	2
sunflower oil	¼ cup
chipotle	12-20 drops
baby spinach	2-4 cups

TIPS

I know what you're thinking ... just throw it all into the pot and it will make a great soup all by itself! That's what I used to do, but found that layering flavours this way creates textures that are impossible if you cook everything at the same time. You will notice the meat is juicy and tender, not overcooked, the vegetables and the beans are cooked to perfection, and the potatoes remain roasted, right in the soup. Perfect for that Olympian in you!

About 10 minutes before the soup is cooked, slice your steak into fine little strips and fry in some sunflower oil.

Sprinkle with sea salt and the chipotle so they are nice and spicy, and only cook until the meat has lost its redness.

Place in a bowl and set aside for garnish. Clean the frying pan to use for the baby spinach.

Rinse the baby spinach and let it wilt at high heat for a few minutes in some water or a little oil in the frying pan. Add to the soup once it is ready. This is the time when you add the extra sunflower oil to give it that extra flavor.

Fill your soup bowls and garnish with the steak and roasted potatoes. Serve with salad and/or fresh whole breads.

"Guaranteed freshness comes from making your own home-made soups and sauces. You know this, when you choose the freshest ingredients packed full of nutrition."

Dad's simple fresh garlic bread

PREP

Serves a family of 4-5
Prep time: 5 minutes
Cooking time: Approx. 3-4 minutes, or until golden

INGREDIENTS

french stick or	1 large
calabrese bread (optional)	1 loaf
fresh garlic	8-12 cloves chopped
sunflower oil	drizzle
sea salt	sprinkle
ground black pepper	sprinkle

TOOLS

1 shallow dish
1 large cookie tray

TIPS

Always try to use a fresh French stick, Calabrese, artisan, or whole grain baguette to make garlic bread. I personally love the fresh bread that toasts up to absolute perfection!

Chop the garlic into small chunky pieces and place in a shallow dish.

Pour some sunflower oil over it and sprinkle with sea salt.

Slice your bread about 1 inch thick, place on the tray and toast one side on broil.

Take them out, turn them over, slather with the garlic mixture, and add pepper.

Return to the oven until golden brown.

For all you garlic lovers! This is the best way to enjoy fresh garlic bread—few things taste better than this!

“My dad was a big believer in fresh garlic. Today I eat it in winter, spring, summer or fall. Just try sourcing local garlic or planting some of your own.”

Sweet potato cuties with proscuitto and dill

PREP

Serves 4-6
Prep time: 10-15 minutes
Cooking time: Approx. 5-8 minutes

INGREDIENTS

sweet potatoes	4 grated
spanish onions	1-2 sliced
proscuitto (nitrate-free)	5 slices
ground pepper	to taste
sunflower oil	drizzle
fresh oregano	to taste
garlic powder	to taste
sea salt	to taste
flour	to sprinkle
fresh dill	for garnish

TOOLS

1-2 frying pans for potatoes

TIPS

Take your time with these! They are delicate and need to be cooked at just the right temperature. Adjust the temperature accordingly. Too high and they will burn. Using sunflower oil and a high, quality ceramic pan makes all the difference in the final outcome.

Grate the sweet potatoes in a bowl. Season with fresh herbs, garlic powder, and sea salt. Sprinkle with flour, combine and set aside.

Fry the onions on high in a little sunflower oil until they are browning and caramelized. Set them aside on a paper towel.

Put sunflower oil into 1 or 2 frying pans. Heat them up to medium.

Pinch the amount you want. A tablespoon or so will make a nice size of appetizer. I use my fingers to select the right amount, and quickly place 3 or 4 in each pan.

Do not flatten them at all; they need a little air and height to look good. Cook on one side until it turns golden, flip and cook the other side.

Each stove cooks differently, so you will have to adjust the heat accordingly.

For the best taste, quickly wipe the pan and refresh the oil between batches.

When cooked, place them on a paper towel to absorb any extra oil.

Once everything is cooked, assemble the appetizers: sweet potatoes first, followed by the caramelized onions.

Top with fresh dill and season with fresh ground pepper.

"These fabulous appetizers are simple, fun to prepare, and full of flavour. They are also show-stoppers and your guests will love them!"

CHANDLER'S

GINGER GOLD

MACINTOSH

Farmers' Markets

Freshness in real time

Beet stars on beet greens with caramelized pumpkin seeds

PREP

Serves a family of 4-6
Prep time: 15 minutes
Cooking time: Approx. 40 minutes

INGREDIENTS

beets with stems and leaves	3-4 large
sea salt	to taste
raw organic pumpkin seeds	½ cup
brandy	splash
garlic cloves	2 chopped
balsamic vinegar	to taste
sunflower oil	to taste

TOOLS

2 large pots
1 frying pan
1 star cookie cutter

TIPS

Beets stain. It's wise to wear disposable gloves to prepare beets. Otherwise you will have pink hands when you're done!

Wash and boil the whole beets until a knife goes in smoothly. Drain and cool.

Peel the cooled beets, cut into round slices, and cut out the stars with a cookie cutter.

Wash and chop the beet leaves and stems. Place them into boiling water. Cook for about 10 minutes separately or until desired tenderness.

Drain and season with salt and chopped garlic in balsamic and sunflower oil dressing.

Plate the greens first and then top with some beet stars.

On high heat toast the pumpkin seeds for a few minutes in a frying pan. Turn off the stove and add the brandy. Turn the stove back on and reduce until the liquid disappears and the seeds are sticky.

Spoon the caramelized pumpkin seeds onto each plated greens and serve!

“Beets are excellent to eat, from top to bottom. I try to plate things so the veggies look appealing. They are eaten more quickly if you get creative with how your food looks!”

Parsnip and potato soup in a pepper squash bowl

PREP

Serves a family of 4-6
Prep time: 10 minutes
Cooking time: Squash Approx. 15 minutes, Soup Approx. 10 minutes

INGREDIENTS

pepper squash	4 in half and cleaned
parsnips	4-5 grated
potatoes	2 peeled
white cooking onion	1 sliced
ground ginger	1 tsp
apple juice	1 cup
sunflower oil	drizzle
sea salt	to taste

TOOLS

1 frying pan
1 pressure cooker
1 metal baking tray or ceramic baking dish
1 hand-held blender

TIPS

Personally I like to fry up a whole parsnip as it tastes great and has a texture like French fries! Being creative with fall squash is fun and entertaining.

Preheat oven to 400°F.

This recipe serves four people but you will have extra soup left over. If you're serving more than four people, cook additional pepper squash.

Cut each pepper squash in half and remove the seeds and stuff so the inside is clean and smooth. Place on the tray, season with salt, drizzle with sunflower oil and cover with foil.

Bake them for 40 minutes, or until you can slide a knife in easily. You can brown them under the broiler if you wish.

Wash, peel, and chop up your potatoes and parsnips, keeping one half of a parsnip aside for garnish. Chop your onions, put them into the pressure cooker first, and start them frying in sunflower oil.

Fry your parsnips with the onions for about 5 minutes. This will increase the natural flavour of the parsnip.

Add the chopped potatoes, ground ginger, apple juice, and just enough water to cover the vegetables, put the lid on the pressure cooker, and cook for 6-8 minutes. When it cools and you release the pressure, remove half the liquid and set it aside.

Purée the soup with a hand-held blender, right in the pressure cooker, adding the liquid back gradually to your desired thickness. I like it really thick! Season to taste.

Your squash should be almost ready and it is time to make your parsnip garnish. Grate the half parsnip and fry it for 2 minutes in a bit of sunflower oil and sea salt.

Take your squash bowls from the oven, let them cool a little, pour in your soup and garnish with the fried parsnip. Garnish with fresh parsley or your favourite herb.

“Fall is a time of plenty and often we don't know what to do with the abundance of squash available. Using them as edible bowls is fun, and no washing dishes is required!”

Fresh curry eggplant tomato sauce on egg noodles

PREP

Serves a family of 4-6
Prep time: 10 minutes
Cooking time: Approx. 15 minutes

INGREDIENTS

spanish onion	1 large sliced
purple eggplant	1 small, 1 large
red tomatoes	3 cubed
yellow tomatoes	2 cubed
orange tomatoes	2 cubed
sunflower oil	for frying
white vinegar	splash
curry	3-5 tsp
ground cloves	¾ tsp
sea salt and ground pepper	to taste
wide egg noodles	5-900 grams

TOOLS

1 pot
1 large deep frying pan

TIPS

I try to select the main ingredients first being local, but when it comes to spices we are limited. Sourcing local do not mean limiting the use of spices.

Clean and chop the eggplants, skin on, into 1 inch cubes.

Wash and chop the tomatoes, skin on, also into 1 inch cubes.

Chop and fry the onion in sunflower oil until it starts to become transparent.

Add the eggplant and continue to fry on medium to high heat, also adding a splash of white vinegar.
You may need to add a little more oil as you go to keep the eggplant moist.

Once the eggplant is half cooked, add your chopped tomatoes. Now add your seasonings, sprinkling a little at a time to suit your taste.

Cook down the tomatoes and they will create their own sauce.

While cooking the sauce is cooking,boil some salted water. Cook the egg noodles for 6-8 minutes, drain well and place on a large serving dish.

Pour the sauce directly onto the noodles and serve! The aroma and colours in this dish are amazing!

“I love coming up with new sauce recipes. This one is simple and easy to make, that has a unique taste that you can create when the farmers' markets are full of fresh produce.”

Getting the family involved in preserving fresh tomatoes

OK, who knows how to make tomato sauce? Who knows how to can tomatoes for winter storage for more sauce? It's a toss up; some of us do and a lot of us don't. But for those who do, it is usually a wonderful family experience on a warm fall day when we can all get together to preserve the tomatoes' full rich flavours for the cold winter months ahead when we will be making lots of pasta and pizzas!

Many people would love to try canning tomatoes but they think it is a lot of work and most novices don't know where to start. To tell the truth, there definitely is work involved, but projects like this can bring families closer together. It is a process with an edible result!

There is no single method carved in stone about how to prepare tomatoes or sauce. We all love to share our ideas and methods. Over the years, my best tips have come from the Italian community; they definitely know their sauce! Chatting with mothers, sisters, cousins, mothers-in-law, friends, co-workers, and even husbands is by far the easiest, most effective way for ideas to come together to create great results.

Today we are happier if we can do things in a timely fashion as we are all very busy. So this year, my mother-in-law and I canned the best tomatoes with less work than we did previously. Traditionally the end result is a sauce with no skins and few seeds, just great tasting sauce. This takes a lot of time and effort. To tighten things up a little and do it quickly with comparable results, we decided to make a few careful shortcuts.

So here it goes!

REQUIRED TOOLS

BURNER (approx. $65 Cdn.) to do this outdoors or in the garage.

LARGE STAINLESS STEEL POT WITH LID for boiling (18" deep).

1 LITRE MASON JARS WITH LIDS Bernardin or Golden Harvest.

CANADIAN JARS for about $9 a dozen. If you can find a small kit, as I did for about $12.00, it has a jar lifter and wide-mouthed funnel for pouring tomatoes or sauce.

4 LARGE BUCKETS for cleaning the tomatoes, and for the cooked tomatoes before peeling.

2 LARGE STAINLESS POTS to put the cooked, peeled tomatoes into before they hit the jars.

CONTAINER for the discarded skins.

STRAINER WITH LONG HANDLE to transfer cooked tomatoes from boiling to cold water.

TONGS for lifting jars from the boiling water (if you don't have a kit).

SOME CLOTHS to mop up messy spills!

WHITE SHEET for cooked jars.

Tomatoes
preserving for the winter

STEP 1: REQUIRED ITEMS
Roughly 60 jars of sauce should be enough for a family of 4 in the winter. This requires approximately 4-5 bushels of tomatoes, the most popular being the plum variety, sea salt, and 2-3 fresh basil plants, washed, dried and leaves pulled from stems.

STEP 2: TOTATO PREP
Always buy your tomatoes 1 week before you are going to can them.

Lay them out on clean cloths, not touching each other, to ripen and prevent bruising. Sort through them and take out questionable ones to use in an immediate sauce.

STEP 3: BOILING AND SKINNING
First clean any dirt off the tomatoes in buckets of water or with the garden hose.

Get the pot of water boiling and add tomatoes to almost fill it, but not boiling over.

Give them time to loosen up from their skins, maybe 10 minutes, depending on how windy it is or if your burner is on high. Keep an eye on all the variables, paying closest attention to the tomatoes themselves.

While they are boiling, you have time to put 2-3 basil leaves in each jar.

Once the tomatoes are ready, they must be put directly into buckets of cold water.

This cools them so you can handle them, and also aids in loosening their skins.

When you can touch them, drain some of the water out of the bucket and remove the skins by hand, discarding them into a container (for the compost).

Toss the skinned tomatoes into a clean stainless pot until full, add a few tablespoons of sea salt, give it a good stir and start filling the jars.

STEP 5: FILLING THE JARS
Fill each jar almost to the top and make sure the rim area where the lid goes is clean. Screw on the top hand tight. Continue until all the jars are filled.

STEP 6: BOILING THE JARS
Rinse the same pot used for the tomatoes and fill it with fresh water. Get the water boiling and then add as many filled jars as will fill the pot, and boil them for 20 minutes. That's it, 20 minutes! Use sturdy tongs to take the jars out of the hot water.

STEP 7: CHECKING ON HOW WELL YOU DID YOUR JOB!
This step is very important. Place all the

HELPFUL TIPS FOR AFTERWARDS

Sometimes we think we have created perfection but we find a flaw or two afterwards. If you find that a jar has not sealed properly, use it right away or freeze it until you need it. Freeze it in a freezer container, not in the jar!

If a lid rises after any time has elapsed, throw out the lid and the tomatoes, as they have been compromised and are inedible, but keep the glass jar for future use. Better to be safe than sorry. Sometimes it happens.

Making your own sauce is miles above the canned or strained type. You will love it and most certainly want to make it a yearly tradition! Whether you want 10 jars that can be done in your kitchen, or 60-100 jars done outside, it is well worth the time and effort, and your family will enjoy the great day spent together. It's that easy!

Good luck! Have fun, and always refer to my site if you have any questions.

jars upside down on a white bed sheet for about 1 day, on a solid table or even on the garage floor where they cannot fall far.

If they are not sealed properly and are going to leak, the sauce will leak out of the top! Also, all the lids should pop down! This is a sign that the seal is perfect! Turn the jars back over, place them in their original packing box, and store them in a cool cellar until you're ready to make that next fabulous dish!

Gettin' saucy
with the family

Ukrainian pork and veal cabbage rolls

PREP

Serves a family of 4-6
Prep time: 15-25 minutes
Cooking time: Approx. 1 to 1½ hours

INGREDIENTS

red cabbage	½ large
green savoy cabbage	½ large

FILLING

ground meat (½ veal, ½ pork)	1 lb
cooking onions	2 medium
tomatoes	4 large
long grain rice	2 cups
sunflower oil	¼ cup
garlic	2 chopped
fresh parsley	¼ cup
fresh thyme	3-4 sprigs
sea salt and pepper	to taste

SAUCE

tomatoes(or 2 jars of sauce)	4-6 fresh (or)
brown sugar	6-8 tbsp
seasonings	to taste
water	1 cup approx.

TOOLS

11 x 15 glass pan
9 x 13 glass pan
1 frying pan
1 large stock pot for cabbage
1 pot for sauce

TIPS

The best cabbage rolls are cooked properly with the right amount of liquid. Add more liquid as they cook down. Try tossing in some Canadian wild rice or using a brown rice mixed in with the scented rice for extra texture.

Preheat the oven to 400°F.

SAUCE

Grate the 4 tomatoes into the pot and bring to a simmer adding the spices.

Add the spices and the brown sugar to the sauce. Simmer while rolling the meat into the cabbage rolls.

CABBAGE

Remove outer leaves and discard. Take apart the cabbage by removing leaves one at a time to avoid tearing.

Into boiling salted water put 5 or so, and cook until they are soft, (do not over cook). Having the leaves separated makes it much easier. Drain and cool in a colander.

RICE AND MEAT FILLING

Chop up the onions. Fry in sunflower oil until transparent, or let them brown a little—creates more flavour. Add the spices while they are cooking.

Add the ground meat and fry until it is half cooked. Then add the rice and grate 4 fresh tomatoes into the meat while simmering.

Stir in ½ cup of water. Let the meat and rice mixture cool.

CONTINUED ON NEXT PAGE

“Creating fresh food that looks colourful and tasty is easy with a little imagination. The little ones love eating colourful healthy foods.”

Ukrainian pork and veal cabbage rolls cont'd

CONTINUED FROM PREVIOUS PAGE

ROLLING THE CABBAGE

Using clean hands, or a tablespoon, put 5-6 tablespoons of meat and rice mixture onto the inner side at the base of the leaf. Fold in the sides and roll to close it up.

Try to be consistent with your cabbage roll size so they cook evenly and look really nice! You can always double up the smaller leaves to keep your rolls the same size.

Fill the glass pan with cabbage rolls, leaving a little space in between them. Drizzle a little sunflower oil over the cabbage rolls, and pour the sauce over them. Add water to cover them completely and sprinkle on a little sea salt and pepper.

Bake at 400°F on the bottom rack for approximately 1 hour, or until the rice is completely cooked.

Halfway through baking, you may need to add a little hot water as the rice will absorb a lot of the water and sauce you started with. Use hot water to prevent breaking the glass pan.

To best judge for the finished dish, always open a cabbage roll from the centre of the pan to see if the rice is cooked and fluffy.

"This is another tasty, low cal comfort food. The flavour always brings me back to when I was small eating them at my grandmother's."

Portabella and sirloin lasagna with fresh oregano and thyme

PREP

Serves a family of 4-6
Prep time: Approx. 30 minutes
Cooking time: Approx. 45 minutes

INGREDIENTS

lasagna **whole wheat** or high quality white	1 package
ground sirloin **or mixed meats:** **½ beef and ½ pork**	1-2 lbs
cooking onions	2 large chopped
garlic	2 cloves
portabella mushrooms	6 chopped
red tomatoes	8 large grated
tomato paste	½ can (78ml)
sunflower oil	½ cup
fresh herbs oregano, thyme	4-6 spigs
salt and pepper	to taste

TOOLS

1 large frying pan
1 large pot for boiling
11 x 15 glass pan

TIPS

For all baked pasta dishes, I prefer to use fresh grated tomatoes. They give a more real taste, with less acidity than canned or bottled tomatoes. Try this recipe with ground chicken or turkey, the taste completely changes.

Preheat oven to 400˚F.

SAUCE

Combine 8 large fresh grated tomatoes with ½ can of tomato paste. Or you can use 2 bottles of your favourite strained tomatoes, season the sauce with fresh herbs, sea salt and pepper.

FILLING

Fry the chopped onions until they caramelize. Add the ground meat and brown it.

Add the ground meat to your your sauce. Cook on medium heat for at least 15 minutes so the flavours combine.

Separately fry the sliced portabella mushrooms brown them well and set aside.

In a large pot, boil water and cook the lasagna as per instructions on the box. Drain and rinse under cool water. Drizzle sunflower oil over the pasta so it doesn't stick together.

Lay the lasagna in the pan, one layer at a time, adding the ground meat with sauce in layers, alternating with layers of mushrooms.

Make sure the top pasta is totally covered with sauce, adding a little water if necessary. Cover with foil.

Bake on the bottom rack for about 45 minutes or until you detect that fantastic aroma!

When baking pasta without cheese, make sure it is wet with liquid while cooking. If needed, add hot water slowly to the pan as it cooks.

"Making lasagna without cheese is simple, and delicious. Once you get the hang of it, you will taste all the natural ingredients you layered inside. You can eat twice as much without the guilt!"

Who knew that with names like these they were not imports?

If you have already breezed though my book, you know that I love mushrooms, specifically fresh, local mushrooms.

Ralph and Julie Baumlisberger of Windy Field Mushrooms have been operating for about five years. It was great to see and learn how mushrooms are grown right here in my own community. This is what I learned...

BLUE OYSTER MUSHROOMS

The process starts with some really good local straw and mycelia (mushroom fungi), black plastic bags, some good packers, and just the right growing conditions. The mycelia are mixed into the straw and packed tightly into black bags with holes punched in them. Then they ride on a cart into a large room where the temperature is 20°C and it is very dark. The internal bag temperature gets hotter than the room and sits at 25°C for three weeks. Then the carts are moved to the growing room where Ralph and Julie turn on all the lights and lower the temperature to 17°C. This drastic change causes the mushrooms to grow. They find their way to the holes and then grow on the outside of the bags! Many mushrooms may grow on one stem, reaching 5-6 inches in height. After about seven to 10 days, enough are ready to be hand picked and delivered to the markets. The bags are returned to the growing room where more mushrooms will sprout out of the holes. This allows them to pick two to three crops before throwing out the bags, mixing a fresh batch of straw and mycelia in new bags, and starting the process all over again.

SHIITAKE MUSHROOMS

These little mushrooms are grown in a similar environment, but on cork-like cubes of compressed sawdust. The cubes are impregnated with both the mycelia and the proper moisture content and spend a 5-month incubation period at the supplier's farm before arriving at Windy Fields Mushrooms. Shiitake mushrooms require more attention than the oyster variety and grow at a slower pace. All of the rooms at Windy Fields Mushrooms are properly vented and temperature controlled with sensors on the doors. They are kept in a growing room at 17°C and take about 7 to 10 days to produce the first crop. Once they are picked, the cubes are cleaned, cut down a little, and soaked in a water bath to rehydrate them. Then they are put back onto the carts in the growing room at 17°C to start the process all over again. Each shipment of blocks produces about three crops of mushrooms that are carefully hand picked and shipped the same day. It is really amazing to look at the tiny new mushrooms that form right after the larger ones are perfect for picking!

Ralph and Julie have taught me that in this country, we can grow wonderful, exceptionally tasty mushrooms, so close to home.

Mushrooms

spending time with the fun guy

Hockley blue oyster and Shiitake mushroom soup

PREP

Serves 4-6
Prep time: 10-15 minutes
Cooking time: Approx. 10-15 minutes

INGREDIENTS

chicken stock	4 cups
Hockley English Ale (optional)	1 can
blue oyster mushrooms	2 cups
Shiitake mushrooms	2 cups
baby 'bellas	2 cups
baby Spanish onions	8 -10
red pepper	1 sliced
garlic cloves	2 chopped
baby spinach	1½ cups
sunflower oil	for frying
sea salt	to taste
fresh ground pepper	to taste

TOOLS

1 large stock pot
1 large frying pan
3 dishes for fried items

TIPS

Some soups need time on the stove to bring out the flavours, and some soups are most tasty when made with ease and in a short time like this one. Use this recipe as a base and, when the season changes, try new and different ingredients. Of course the ale is optional, you can always replace equal amount with chicken stock.

Why should we use the frying pan when making soup? Frying things individually brings out the full flavour of each ingredient. Adding these colourful items at the end maintains their visual appeal and keeps their great taste.

Start by putting the chicken stock and beer into the pot. Set on medium heat to cook out the beer, just a little, at a low boil for about 5 minutes.

Wash, slice and measure the 3 types of mushrooms. Clean and slice the onions and red pepper. Chop the garlic cloves. Set aside.

First fry the garlic and mushrooms in sunflower oil on high heat, so they brown. Remove from the pan and set aside.

Do the same with the slices of red pepper, but only fry for a few minutes to keep them firm, not soft. A little browning is good. Remove from the pan and set aside.

Wilt the spinach in the pan and set aside.

Toss the mushrooms into the stock pot and continue to simmer for 3-5 minutes.

Gently fry the onions, keeping them nicely together as shown in the image.

Turn off the stock pot and add all the rest of the ingredients, except for the fried onions. Season to taste and serve with the onions as a garnish.

"I decided to create a sexy soup that would knock your man's socks off with loads of flavour! Using a really great local beer that is layered with flavour adds to the great taste."

Eggplant and 'bella mushroom pie

PREP

Serves 4-6
Prep time: 20 minutes
Cooking time: frying time Approx. 15 minutes
Oven time Approx. 1 hour

INGREDIENTS

SAUCE	
fresh tomatoes - grated	6 large (or chopped)
strained tomatoes	1 jar
water	1-2 cups
fresh oregano	2 sprigs
fresh garlic cloves	2 chopped
sea salt and pepper	to taste
garlic powder	2 tsp
EGGPLANT AND MUSHROOMS	
baby portabella mushrooms	2 x 227 grams
sunflower oil	for frying
large purple eggplants	1-2
washed spinach for layering	4-6 cups
COATING	
flour	½ cup
eggs for wash	3-4 beaten
whole wheat crackers	2 bags
seasoning for crackers	2 tbsp chicken soup

soup base, garlic powder, fresh oregano, fresh thyme, sea salt and pepper

TOOLS

1 pot
3 shallow bowls
2 frying pans
drying rack
11 x 15 glass baking dish

TIPS

Layering is the key to making this great dish, but not too heavy on the sauce. It's a great opportunity to taste the vegetables, and you want it to retain its shape when cut for appealing presentation.

Preheat oven to 400°F.

Start by letting your sauce simmer for ½ hour to cook down while you prepare the rest.

First, slice the mushrooms. Fry them in sunflower oil until they brown. Set aside.

Put the flour in one bowl. Prepare the egg wash in the second bowl. Crush the crackers by hand, put them into the third bowl and add the seasonings a little at a time and re-season as necessary.

Slice the eggplants horizontally into round discs - half inch thick slices. Coat them one at a time in the flour, then the egg wash, and then the cracker coating.

Fry them in sunflower oil at medium to high heat until golden brown and crunchy. Set them on a drying rack until you're done. If your oil gets dirty or has brown bits floating in it, discard it, wipe the pan, and replace with fresh oil.

Once you finish frying all the eggplant slices, use the pan to wilt the spinach for a few minutes in some oil. Set it aside for assembly.

Note: Save a good portion of the mushrooms to use for the top layer.

The bottom layer is sauce. Lay eggplant slices into the dish to start one layer. Pour sauce over the egg plant, sprinkle with mushrooms, and add a layer of spinach. Repeat layering with eggplant, sauce, mushrooms and spinach until the tray is full. Add enough in each layer to keep it from drying. Keep some sauce for serving.

Bake for an hour, checking to make sure it cooks through.

Château des Charmes Estate Bottled Cabernaet-Merlot, VQA Niagara-on-the-Lake

Cab Merlot
Beaulolais Cru-Chiroubles, Fleurie or St. Amour- Franc
or de Heuvel Pinotage - South Africa

“My goal was to make a lasagna with no pasta, no cheese and totally vegetarian. I believe I have succeeded as my family loves this dish! I am certain you will enjoy it as much as we do.”

Cumin pork rib roast with homemade applesauce

PREP

Serves a family of 4-6
Prep time: 10-15 minutes
Cooking time: Roast time Approx. 3.½ hours
Veggies Approx. 10-15 minutes

INGREDIENTS

pork rib roast	1 any size
canadian white wine	1 bottle
potatoes	4 large cut as shown
carrots	2 large curt as shown
rutabaga	½ cut as shown
arugula	2 cups
sunflower oil	for frying
APPLESAUCE	2 peeled
green delicious apples	½-1 cup
apple juice or water	2 tsp
cinnamon	drizzle
maple syrup	
RIB COATING	1 tsp
cumin	1 tsp
sea salt	1 tsp
garlic powder	1 tsp
pepper	drizzle
maple syrup	

TOOLS

1 roasting pan
1 bowl
1 frying pan or pot
hand-held blender

TIPS

Be generous with the spices in this dish; it is meant to be bold and flavourful!

Preheat oven to 400°F.

Applesauce may be made ahead of time or while the roast is cooking. Peel, core and cut the apples into quarters.

Cook with cinnamon in a frying pan or pot, adding water or juice as needed, until tender. Purée with a hand-held blender and set aside.

Coat your ribs with the seasonings, drizzle on maple syrup, pour your wine into the pan, and bake uncovered for about 20 minutes to seal the roast. Then cover with foil or a lid.

In order to get your pork tender, you must cook it long and slow. Keep checking on liquid levels, adding water as you go so it does not dry out.

About an hour before the roast will be ready, clean and peel your vegetables, cutting them into half-inch rectangular sticks. Set them in a bowl of cold water.

Dry first on a paper towel and start to cook them 10-15 minutes before the meat is ready, also knowing the meat will need to rest 5-10 minutes before being cut.

Put sunflower oil in the pan, and fry the vegetable sticks on medium heat, turning them as they brown.

Add the fresh applesauce over the meat and drizzle with maple syrup. This makes a fantastic fall dinner!

Château des Charmes Estate Bottled Barrel Fermented Chardonnay, VQA Niagara-on-the-Lake

Chardonnay Sauvignon Blanc
Andert or Wollmuth from Austria, Castelo de Medina, Spain.

“Local and antibiotic-free pork is an option for a better cut of meat, excellent when cooked with fresh in-season apples and root vegetables.”

Baked eggplant sauce for meats and vegetables

PREP

Serves a family of 4-6
Prep time: 15 minutes
Cooking time: Approx. 30 minutes

INGREDIENTS

eggplants	4-6 small peeled
chickpeas	¼ cup rinsed
garlic	2 cloves chopped
sunflower oil	½ cup
white vinegar	¼ cup
lemon	½
garlic powder	2 tsp
sea salt	to taste
fresh ground pepper	to taste

TOOLS

1 baking tray
1 bowl
hand-held blender

TIPS

Always try to adjust your salt slowly, garlic powder has a salty taste all on its own without added salt. If you like a thicker sauce, add another 1/4 cup of chickpeas.

Preheat oven to 425°F.

Bake the eggplants whole, with skins on, for up to a half hour, or until cooked.

Remove from the oven and let cool. Then remove the insides from their skins.

Put the eggplants into a bowl with the chickpeas and chopped garlic. Add the liquids and blend with the garlic powder, sea salt and pepper to taste.

This is a great sauce for fall when barbecuing fall veggies and goes well with souvlaki, as a bread dipper and so much more.

Really easy—really great taste!

“I enjoy eating healthy sauces that you can make at home using local in-season vegetables. They taste great, don't have artificial flavours, sugars and other additives!”

Baked Cornish hen with spinach pasta and rhubarb

PREP

Serves 4-6
Prep time: 10 minutes
Cooking time: Approx. 45 minutes

INGREDIENTS

Cornish hens	2 washed
STUFFING	
fresh baguette	½ chopped cubes
small Spanish onion	1 chopped
ground sage	1 tsp
garlic powder	1 tsp
sea salt and pepper	to taste
egg	1 beaten
celery deveined	1 chopped
apple juice or chicken stock	½ cup
sunflower oil	for pasta
spinach pasta	3-500 grams
fresh or frozen rhubarb	2 cups
fresh cranberries	1 cup
maple syrup (or cane sugar)	½ cup

TOOLS

1 large oven tray for hens
1 large pot for pasta
1 pot for rhubarb

TIPS

Try stuffing the smaller birds, and making the stuffing from scratch. It is so simple and very tasty, and you can develop your own flavours by changing up the spices you use.

Preheat oven to 375°F.

Start by making the stuffing. Cut up the baguette into small pieces, chop up the Spanish onions and celery and add to the bread along with the beaten egg and spices. Add the liquid and mix by hand.

Stuff the rinsed hens and season with sea salt and pepper. Cover and put in oven and bake for about 40 minutes, depending on the size of the hens.

About 15 minutes before they are ready, boil salted water and cook the spinach pasta 7-10 minutes. Rinse and drizzle with sunflower oil.

In another pot, add the rhubarb, cranberries and the maple syrup, cook down just enough to cook the rhubarb for five minutes or so. Try not to overcook the rhubarb or it will fall apart.If you cook from frozen it will retain its shape.

Remove hens for the oven when cooked. If they need browning, put them under the broiler for about 5 minutes to brown.

Cut them in half and plate on the spinach pasta. Pour the sauce over the hen and serve.

"Cornish hens are tasty birds. Stuff them and accent them with any in-season fruit and really great spices. Simple, easy and tastes great!"

Light, tasty and incredibly delicious: sunflower oil

We grow beautiful sunflowers and produce some of the best sunflower oil in North America.

Since Anastasia was allergic to olive oil as a baby, I needed to find a really good replacement. After trying various oils I decided it was going to be the one.

I find that sunflower enhances food's natural flavour and fries, bakes and cooks without an aftertaste. It is very light and tasty. Sunflower oil has a higher amount of Vitamin E than any vegetable oil and has been found to be low in saturated fat levels. I can also cook at fairly high temperatures without much difficulty.

My whole family loves the taste. We use it mixed with garlic and balsamic to dip our fresh bread it. Instead of using margarine, drizzle sunflower oil on our toast in the morning with a just a sprinkle of sea salt. Since it is so light in taste, we eat it often, without any concerns.

I use sunflower oil in baking cakes, muffins and cookies and find the textures are wonderful, the taste is great and everything has that lightness about it once baked.

It is perfect for roasting, frying and just about anything you cook.

One of the reasons many of us are probably not buying it yet, is that it is a little higher in price than canola and vegetable oil. However, if you compare the cost of olive oil, it ends up being less. This does not concern me as I feel I am paying for a higher quality oil. I also have recognized that it is grown and produced here in North America.

Sunflowers are a very interesting crop to grow as they grow well in areas that get little precipitation and grow in soils that are well drained. For farmlands that have been eroded and retain very little moisture, this is a perfect crop to grow.

Sunflowers also produce delicious seeds, which are very nutritious and make an absolutely yummy snack. Any seeds that are too small are packaged for birdseed.

Try using sunflower oil if you're looking to give a boost to the natural flavours in vegetables and salads or are looking for a great substitute for margarine-based products.

I would highly recommend using sunflower oil in your day-to-day cooking and baking.

It makes everything taste fantastically delicious! If your looking to go local with your oil, this one just might be for you. Move over olive oil!

Sunflower oil has a higher amount of Vitamin E than any vegetable oil and has been found to be low in saturated fat levels

Sunflower oil

for the sun lover in you

Fabulous spinach and meat pie

PREP

Serves a family of 4-6
Prep time: 30 minutes
Cooking time: Approx. 45 minutes give or take

INGREDIENTS

phyllo pastry	1 package
fresh spinach	1-2 bunches
onion yellow or white	1 large chopped
scallions use the green and white	3 sliced
lean ground beef/pork	1-1½ lbs
scented long grain ricew	1 cup
wild Canadian rice	1 cup
fresh dill	½ bunch chopped
chicken stock or soup base for additional flavour in the rice	½-1 cup
sunflower oil	½ cup
salt and pepper	to taste

TOOLS

1 or 2 large frying pans
1 pot for boiling
pastry brush and a glass for oiling the phyllo
11x15 glass pan

TIPS

Precooking your ingredients separately lets you layer your dish for a more appetizing finished appearance—way more appealing than just a mixture! My personal favourite phyllo is President's Choice®—it is light, flaky and tasty. Oil every single sheet of your phyllo lightly—too much will make it too oily, not enough and it will be dry. The kids love the phyllo, so do not be surprised if the first few times you make this dish they want to eat the crunchy phyllo first!

Preheat oven to 375°F.

Cook scented and wild rice together, using just enough chicken stock/soup base and water to make the end result fluffy.

Wash the spinach thoroughly, cut into small pieces and set aside.

Chop the onion into small pieces and fry in sunflower oil, allowing it to caramelize. Then add the spinach and chopped scallions, cooking just until they wilt. Add fresh chopped dill, salt and pepper. Set this aside in a dish if you need the same pan for the meat.

Fry the ground meat until almost done, making sure it's brown and retains moisture. Drain excess oil from the meat and set it aside.

Open your phyllo but ahead of time, as you want it to be easy to work with, nto dry out. Take half of the phyllo and, using sunflower oil, spread each sheet individually into the large glass pan, lightly brushing oil on every sheet.

For the middle of the pie, spread out the rice, the ground meat, the spinach, scallion, onion and dill mixture.

Lay on most of the remaining phyllo, brushing each layer with oil as you go. There will be excess phyllo hanging over the sides, so just fold it into the pie making a border.

CONTINUES ON NEXT PAGE

"Spinach and meat pie is on top of the favourites list in my house. A dish like this makes snacking really easy for the kids when they come home from school."

Fabulous spinach and meat pie cont'd

CONTINUED FROM PREVIOUS PAGE

If you find the ends of the phyllo get dry, just trim them off and then fold the ends into the sides of the dish, making sure you brush with oil so it cooks up nice and crunchy!

Before placing the pie in the oven, cut it into triangles with a sharp serrated knife.

Brush the entire top of the pie with sunflower oil. Sometimes I like to sprinkle sea salt and fresh ground pepper over the top, it creates more flavor and looks really nice.

Cook the pie in the middle of the oven for about 45 minutes so the phyllo cooks evenly on top and bottom. Golden is what you're looking for.

"Once a Greek traditional spinach pie, this is a healthier, more fulfilling version for those who are watching their calorie and dairy intake, but love the traditional taste."

Roasted stuffed peppers and eggplants with fresh tomatoes

PREP

Serves a family of 4-6
Prep time: 20 minutes
Cooking time: Approx. 1 to 1½ hours

INGREDIENTS

peppers yellow, orange and red	6 large cleaned
eggplant	1 large or 3 small
tomatoes	3 large grated
ground meat	1lb
½ lean veal and ½ pork	
chicken stock	1-2 cups
scented long grain rice	1 cup
sunflower oil	¼ cup
fresh parsley	2-4 tsp
fresh oregano or dried	2-4 tsp
salt and pepper	to taste

TOOLS

11 x 5 glass pan
1 frying pan
blender
grater

TIPS

Try stuffing eggplants, zucchini's and tomatoes using the same ingredients and follow the same instructions and you have a brand new dish!

Preheat oven to 425°F.

Cut tops off peppers, ½ inch down, use the tops as lids. Clean out the insides out of the including the white flesh.

Cut the eggplant(s). Scoop out the insides and toss into the blender for adding back into the final filling mixture.

Fry the onions in sunflower oil until they just start to caramelize.

Add the ground meat and fry until almost cooked, with the herbs and spices. Use a hand grinder to grate the tomatoes, skin and all, onto the meat. Add mashed eggplant and the rice, simmer for a few minutes, remove from stove.

Then add chicken stock to make sure the filling is moist, so the rice absorbs the water.

Stuff the peppers filling them to the top, put their tops on, and sit them upright in the pan. Drizzle them with sunflower oil. Add 1 inch of water to the bottom of the pan.

Bake at 425˚F and keep checking for the rice to fluff up nicely.

If they look dry, add hot water directly into the peppers—or drizzle some over them.

They should start to brown and collapse a little as they soften up while cooking.

Cooking time depends on the rice, so lift a pepper lid to see if the rice is fully cooked.

“Fresh stuffed peppers make great summer or fall dishes: simple, full of flavour, and baked all in one dish! How fresh is that?”

The changes facing the North American grocery landscape

I am a firm believer that a grocery store should be about local fruits and vegetables, fresh local meats, fish and poultry. It is really nice to see foods that are locally produced, and are available to me so I can support my community. Let's get back to the way things used to be.

I am a huge fan of grocery stores that support local. So it would make sense for me to talk about my local grocery stores and share with you how wonderful they make my grocery store shopping experiences.

In my community we are so fortunate that we have a wonderful family based grocery store called Garden Foods. They have been in business since 1972 and owned by the Carbone family. The prices are always fair, the quality is unbeatable and they support the local farmers as well. They make a point of purchasing the food as if they were putting it on their own table. You cannot beat that.

In our community, we also have an array of large grocery retailers that are supporting local as well. Some of them are bigger supporters than others. It is our repsonsibility to recognize what grocery stores are doing their best to offer us the most local food choices, with an emphasis on fresh.

We have a surplus of fine grocery stores available to us in our local area as you may have in yours. There has been a definite movement to keep competing globally, which in turn has changed the grocery store shopping landscape, from what it was.

There are a few that stand above the rest because they concentrate on offering the freshest local fruits, vegetables and local meats and poultry. This is really what a grocery store should be—all about fresh and local.

As consumers, we have fallen into a state of convenience, and have assisted in changing what the grocery store carries.

If we are interested in supporting local through large grocery retailers, we should be shopping at those who cater to your wants and needs. They will be quite happy to accommodate as you and I are very important to them.

So how do you know where to shop? Well, to me it is not all about price or quantity. It is about how real the food is, where it comes from and how fresh it is. And let's not forget the more local and in-season, the better.

It is extremely important that we keep true to our small and large local grocery retailers that fairly support local vendors. This ensures that the best foods will be available to you and I for many years to come. We will be supporting our own economy and keeping our hard earned dollars locally to be used to put us back to work.

'Fokas' on local

getting to know your grocery options

Fall stuffed pumpkins with penne and sirloin

PREP

Serves a family of 4-6
Prep time: 20-30 minutes
Baking time: Approx. 40 minutes

INGREDIENTS

pumpkins	4-6 small cleaned
spanish onions	2 sliced
sunflower oil	to taste
ground sirloin	1-1½lbs
garlic	2 cloves chopped
sea salt and pepper	to taste
plum tomatoes	1 large jar
penne	500 grams
thyme and oregano (fresh)	to taste

TOOLS

1 frying pan
1 pot
1-2 large baking dishes
hand-held blender
foil

TIPS

My little ones love to sort though the messy pumpkin and remove the tiny seeds. Then we bake them in the oven until they are brown, and season with salt. They are the best pumpkins seeds to eat whole as they are delicate and tasty!

Preheat oven to 425°F.

For this recipe there is flexibility with the ingredients. Pumpkins vary in size so the amounts to fill them will be different.

Gauging the pasta amount is done visually. I usually use a couple handfuls of pasta per pumpkin and up to a ¼lb. of meat.

Cut the tops off the pumpkins, 1½ inches down, and keep them for the lids. Remove the seeds and innards and sit the pumpkins in the pans to wait for the filling.

Fry the chopped onions in sunflower oil, then add the chopped garlic and ground sirloin and brown it, adding seasonings. Make sure the meat stays moist.

To make your sauce, put the plum tomatoes into a pot and blend them. Add your herbs and spices and simmer for about 10 minutes to infuse the flavours.

Add the sauce to the meat mixture, stir in the uncooked penne, and add enough water for the pasta to absorb while cooking. Remove from the stove and fill the pumpkins.

Replace the tops and cover each pumpkin with foil. Add 1 inch or so of water to the bottom of the dish and place in the oven.

Bake for up to 40 minutes, gauging by the softness of the pumpkins and whether the pasta inside is fully cooked.

"Tiny pumpkins are perfect for stuffing full of your favourite pasta and meat; a really simple and tasty dish everyone will love!"

Kids' veggie wedges with creamy baked veggie dips

PREP

Serves a family of 4-6
Prep time: 15-20 minutes
Cooking time: Approx. 35-40 minutes

INGREDIENTS

beets	3-4 peeled
carrots	2-3 peeled
parsnips	2 peeled
sweet potato	1 large
turnips	4 small
rutabaga	½ peeled
sunflower oil	for baking
cane sugar	sprinkling
sea salt	to taste
sunflower oil	¼ cup

TOOLS

1 large glass baking dish
1 smaller glass baking dish for beets
1 small ceramic or glass baking dish for scraps
2 bowls for sauces
hand-held blender

TIPS

Trying new winter vegetables like these makes eating them a lot more fun and exciting! Baking the veggies keeps them looking and tasting real, the kids will love them!

Preheat oven to 400°F.

Often we do not know what else to do with fall vegetables so we just boil and mash them. But they are incredible when baked in a pan, seasoned lightly and oiled!

They're also fun eating for the kids. The key is to make colourful pieces into interesting shapes that are small enough for a toddler's tiny hand, easy for them to eat independently, yet packed full of nutrition.

Quantities listed (left) are just guidelines. It depends on the size of the pan. You must lay the veggies side by side, not overlapping, so when plating them for the kids they easily retain their shape.

Remember to use gloves when peeling and cutting the beets to avoid stained hands! Peel and cut the uncooked beets into ¼ inch slices, then cut the slices into shapes. Place them neatly in the smaller baking dish, with no water, and drizzle with oil.

Clean, peel and cut the other veggies into shapes—stars, squares, triangles, circles, rectangular sticks, etc. Lay them carefully, side by side, in the large pan, drizzle with sunflower oil, sprinkle with sea salt and cane sugar, and add ½ inch of water.

Put the leftover veggie pieces (no beets!) into a separate baking dish. Drizzle with oil, sprinkle with sea salt and cane sugar, and add ½ inch of water. Cover all 3 dishes with tin foil. Bake them for about 35-40 minutes.

CONTINUES ON NEXT PAGE

“I was inspired to make fun squash shapes and really colourful dips for the kids to enjoy!”

Kids' veggie wedges with creamy baked veggie dips cont'd

PREP

Serves a family of 4-6
Prep time: 5 minutes for dips

INGREDIENTS

DIPS	
beets	2 medium
veggie peices	2 cups
chickpeas	¼ cup per dip
maple syrup	to taste

TOOLS

1 pot
2 bowls
1 hand-held blender
2 little serving dishes

TIPS

To introduce new vegetables to the little ones, cook one new vegetable at a time to find out what they prefer and eliminate those that they truly do not like. Make it fun—they will love it!

CONTINUED FROM PREVIOUS PAGE

When cooked, remove the pan of beets and the smaller pan of bits from the oven. Turn on the broiler and broil the large pan of veggie shapes until browning appears. Once browned, but definitely not too soft, remove from the oven and let cool.

While they are cooling you can make the dips. The pink dip is made from beets and the orange dip is the mixed veggie bits from cutting the shapes! Really simple and really fun!

HOT PINK DIP

Peel and boil 2 beets until a knife goes in smoothly. Drain away most of the water, leaving some in with the beets. Purée with ¼ cup of chickpeas, adding 1 tbsp of sunflower oil, and sea salt to taste. You may add maple syrup to make a sweeter taste if you wish. Pour into a bowl for dipping.

SUNNY ORANGE DIP

Purée the leftover bits of the veggies in a bowl with ¼ cup of chickpeas, adding 1 tbsp of sunflower oil and sea salt to taste. To sweeten, add some maple syrup. Pour into tiny bowls for dipping.

Totally tasty, visually pleasing—with colourful choices, you may get them hooked! They will never know how healthy it is!

“I found that cutting the vegetables into shapes, the right size for the kids to hold in their hands, and plating them in a fun way, they really do enjoy eating them!”

Fresh apples are perfect for the long winter season ahead

At this time of year we are experiencing those chilly nights and if we're lucky, the leaves have just started to turn all of their magnificent fall colours - red, yellow and my personal favourite, orange. What a wonderful and bountiful place to live, with all the local fall produce being picked from the fields!

The farmers' markets are buzzing with excitement, and the local grocery stores are packed from floor to ceiling with the freshest local produce you can find. There is no shortage of great-tasting food, as you probably have your favourite vegetables and fruits ready for harvest in your community.

It's another great excuse to get the kids in the car, go off on an adventure and go apple picking! I personally love to visit and chat with local people, talk about what is current and buy the freshest local produce available.

I have three 150-year-old apple trees on my property and we get a few good apples from them. I haven't figured out just how to manage them yet; this will come of course. But in the short-term, having a wonderful apple orchard 15 minutes away is good enough for us!

Nearby, Albion Apple Orchard is in their 14th year growing apples and a wonderful country market full of locally produced, homemade sauces, jams, soups, pies, hot apple cider and of course apples!

Scott, the owner, has roughly 30 different varieties of fruit trees and 22 of them are apples - Gala, Spartan and Idared, to name just a few. A new variety that he has this year is the totally delicious Honey Crisp. My personal favourite that I tried at the orchard two years ago when my daughter was on a school trip, is the Empire. This apple is a cross between a Macintosh and a Delicious and what an apple it is - juicy and tangy - perfect for eating right off the tree.

Farmers' markets are buzzing with excitement and local grocery stores are packed

---

If you live in Canada or the upper USA, you probably have a farm right in your own backyard that produces fruits and vegetables for you to pick yourself. Why not check it out?

You can pick your own, grab yourself a bag and go apple picking. Some trees are a perfect height for the kids while others require a ladder.

There are many great apple orchards like this one, so why not support local and make a day out of it? We do and the kids love it!

Apples

sweet, juicy and delicious!

Pulled chicken and apple butternut squash soup

PREP

Serves 4-6
Prep time: 10 minutes
Cooking time: Approx. 10-15 minutes

INGREDIENTS

chicken breasts	2 sliced
medium butternut squash	1 (6 cups chopped)
chicken stock	4 cups
large Empire apples	2 peeled
ground sage	1-2 tsp
sea salt	to taste
scallions	2 sliced
sunflower oil	drizzle

TOOLS

large pot
small pot
hand-held blender

TIPS

Try cooking your meats separately and adding them just before serving. This makes for tender, mouthwatering results. I like the pulled chicken in this soup; it has a more genuine chicken texture than when cut into cubes.

This one is really easy!

Peel the squash, cut into cubes and set aside.

Toss the whole chicken breasts into a small pot of salted boiling water and cook until the pink is gone from their centre.

Remove them from the water and set aside.

Pour the water from the chicken into the large pot, add the chicken stock and bring to a boil.

Peel and chop the apples and toss into the soup. Add the butternut squash, keeping 2 cups aside. As the soup is cooking, add sage and sea salt to taste.

Cook the 2 cups of squash separately in fresh water in the small pot. Boil for about 10 minutes or until the squash is soft - it must stay firm enough to retain its cube shape. Drain and set aside.

Blend the large pot of soup until creamy.

Pull the chicken apart, ripping it so it has texture and the pieces are small enough to fit on a spoon. Add it to the soup along with the separately boiled squash.

Serve in soup bowls. Garnish with chopped scallions and a drizzle of sunflower oil!

“Nothing beats the texture of pulled chicken pieces in a tasty soup. Apples and squash complement each other quite nicely.”

Roasted Muscovy duck with pear and spelt linguini

PREP

Serves a family of 8
Prep time: 15 minutes
Cooking time: Approx 4½ hours

INGREDIENTS

male muscovy duck	5-7lb
soya sauce	¼ cup
ground cinnamon	2 tbsp
sea salt	sprinkle the duck
dark brown sugar	½ to ¾ cup
ground ginger	1 tsp
white wine	1 bottle
cinnamon sticks	3 whole
yellow onions	3 small
medium pears	6 halved
star anises	3-5
fresh chopped walnuts	1/4 cup
spelt linguini	500 grams
garlic cloves	4-6
sunflower oil	drizzle
fruit flavored liqueur	generous splash

TOOLS

1 roasting pan
1 frying pan for reduction
1 pot for pasta

TIPS

The real secret behind a great tasting duck that is moist and juicy is to split the duck in half, breast side up, lay in a baking tray and rub sea salt all over it. A half a cup or so will do .Let sit overnight until ready to cook the next day. Rinse, season and roast.

Château des Charmes Estate Bottled Gamay Noir,
VQA Niagara-on-the-Lake

Gamay
Côte du Rhone, France
Plan de Dieu Promenade des Princes or Lavau Cairanne

Preheat oven to 425°F.

Wash your duck, let it get to room temperature, and tie up its legs and wings.

In the roasting pan, marinate the duck all over with soya sauce. Season it well with the ground cinnamon, sea salt, brown sugar and ginger. Give the duck a good rub with those spices!

Add the white wine to the pan, plus cinnamon sticks, onions and star anises. Put the duck into the oven, uncovered, for 15 minutes just to seal the skin. Then cover with foil (or roasting pan lid) and bake.

Cooking time depends on your taste and the amount of tenderness you desire. Some butchers will tell you 15-20 minutes per pound. However, I cook mine for 30-40 minutes per pound.

Wash the pears, cut them into halves, remove the centres, and leave the skins on. Put them in during the last hour before the duck is done.

In a pot of salted boiling water, cook your linguini for 8-10 minutes. Chop your garlic fine and sprinkle on the cooked linguini, along with sunflower oil and sea salt. Use the drippings to drizzle over linguini before serving.

Toss your walnuts into a hot pan, with a generous splash of your favorite liqueur (fruit flavoured is nice) and reduce until the walnuts are sticky and coated just right.

Use a few of the pears and the juice of the duck to make a pear reduction. Serve with the pears and spelt linguini, drizzled with the pear reduction.

Perfect for the whole family—sweet and delicious! Well worth the wait!

"Fresh duck is definitely not eaten often enough. Yes, the skin is inedible, but the meat is truly lean and delicious if cooked long enough. Sweet, sour or spicy, it's the cook in you that makes all the difference!"

Rosemary roasted leg of of lamb with purple plums and chive flowers

PREP

Serves a family of 4-6
Prep time: 15 minutes
Cooking time: Approx. 3-4 hours

INGREDIENTS

lamb	1 large leg
white vinager	¼ cup
garlic powder	sprinkle
sea salt	sprinkle
ground pepper	sprinkle
thyme fresh	a couple of sprigs
sunflower oil	drizzle
white wine	1 bottle
red plums	6-12 skins on
purple chive flowers	3-4
potatoes	6 peeled
sea salt	to taste
plain soya milk	¼ cup
sunflower oil	¼ cup
chive flowers	3-4

TOOLS

1 large roasting pan
1 large pot for potatoes

TIPS

The purpose of using vinegar is to improve the taste of the lamb. You will be pleasantly surprised if you have not used this technique before.

Château des Charmes Estate Bottled Cabernet Franc, VQA Niagara-on-the-Lake

Cab Franc Chateauneuf du Pape, Domaine du Grand Tinel, Domaine de Chanssaud, Domaine Saint Michel-Rhone Valley France

Preheat oven to 400°F.

Wash the leg of lamb well with vinegar, salt and water. This will make the lamb taste really nice.

Rinse and put into the pan. Sprinkle with garlic powder, sea salt, and freshly ground pepper, and rub all over. Pinch your thyme apart and lay it under and on top of the leg.

Drizzle with sunflower oil and pour the wine around the leg—do not pour on top of it.

Bake uncovered until the skin is seared, for about ½ hour at 400°F. Reduce temperature to 375°F and continue cooking.

Cover with foil and bake for another 3 hours at least, depending on your oven.

Add your plums for the final 30 minutes.

About 1 hour before the lamb is cooked, add your peeled potatoes to salted boiling water. Boil until desired tenderness and then mash adding the soya, oil and sea salt. Add the chive flowers just before serving.

Check to make sure that the meat looks soft and will come off the bone easily. Looking for the meat that wants to come away from the leg is a very good sign it is done!

Use the drippings to make spectacular sauce!

This is a perfect spring dish served with mashed potatoes topped with fresh purple chive flowers.

“I used a local, fresh leg of lamb for this recipe, with local plums, and purple chives from my garden. It is easy to locate really good food close to home.”

Elk liver with onions and fresh veggies

PREP

Serves a family of 4
Prep time: 15-20 minutes
Cooking time: Approx. 8 minutes

INGREDIENTS

elk livers	4 fresh
broccoli	1 full head
cauliflower	½ head
Spanish onion	1 large sliced
light soya sauce	2 tsp
sunflower oil	for frying
sea salt	to taste
ground black pepper	to taste
fresh parsley	garnish

TOOLS

1 frying pan
1 pot

TIPS

Why not try cooking liver with soya sauce? It changes the taste and brings the liver to a new flavour level. You might be surprised at the kids reaction when they eat it cooked this way. It certainly goes over well in my house, so give it a try.

Clean your vegetables first, cut into tiny florets, and rinse in salted water.

Fry the sliced onion in sunflower oil on medium heat until browned.

Add soya sauce, sea salt and the livers. Fry at medium heat for about 4 minutes on each side.

Blanch your veggie florets for a few minutes in salted boiling water.

Plate the elk liver and veggies drizzled with sunflower oil sprinkled with pepper.

This dish is packed full of nutrition! If you want a sauce or reduction, try using a beef stock, thicken and drizzle over the liver.

"Amazingly there are a lot of people who love liver. A healthier more natural cut may be a great way for us all to get the flavour we love. !"

Elk sausage with shredded potatoes and fried mushrooms

PREP

Serves a family of 4-6
Prep time: 15 minutes
Cooking time: Approx. 15-20 minutes

INGREDIENTS

elk sausages fresh local	4-6
potatoes	2-4 grated
white mushrooms	8 oz sliced
dill fresh	for garnish
sunflower oil	for frying
sea salt and pepper	to taste

TOOLS

2 frying pans

TIPS

Try to source local farmers who sell organic products. Grazed and grain-fed meats definitely have a better taste. Large-scale farming does not give you the same quality meat. Be adventurous and try local wild boar, grazed beef and pork, organically raised lamb.

Château des Charmes Gamay Noir 'Droit',
St. David's Bench Vineyard,
VQA St. David's Bench

Gamay Noir
Cab Merlot or Cabernet Franc
ViewPointe Winery, Ontario North Shore Lake Erie

Peel and grate (shred) the potatoes. Sit them in salted water until it's time to cook them.

Fry your elk sausages first, in a little sunflower oil, on medium heat. This meat is lean and takes 10-15 minutes at the most to brown.

Remove the sausages from the pan, and set aside, keeping them warm.

Fry the sliced mushrooms in the same pan on high heat until nice and brown. The full flavour comes out this way, and you lose very little moisture and retain the full flavour.

Drain the water from the potatoes, heat the other frying pan, and drizzle with oil. Fry the potatoes until browned, seasoning with sea salt, pepper, and chopped dill.

Serve by placing a handful of fried potatoes on each plate, topped with slices of elk sausage and fried mushrooms.

“Elk sausages are lean and taste fantastic! Trying meats that are not commercially grown gives you the opportunity to taste the difference.”

All good reasons to choose local, naturally raised beef

It is really important to me that I source my beef locally. There is a wonderful farm not too far from me that allows their animals to graze in the fields and live a stress-free life.

Cows are curious creatures, with clear eyes filled with pure innocence and trust; kind of like children. Although they remain cautious and watch for your next move, they live well in their natural environment. This idyllic setting is a far cry from commercial farming.

Bill, Wendy, James and Nathan Masters of Knollbrook Farm live and work on their farm. They are humble people who seem to have a great amount of respect for the animals they raise. All of the animals are processed in government-inspected facilities. There is a huge difference between the quality of a naturally raised animal compared to commercially produced beef.

What seems to be holding back a small farmer like this (who wants to expand and grow) is a thing called "quota." This policy is a very sensitive subject with farmers and, in my opinion, it has damaged local farmers because it allows the free flow of imported meats. This quota policy also makes it almost too expensive for young farmers to get into the beef producing business.

By supporting local beef producers we will der get the best quality meat to our table—pastured, free of antibiotics, and hormones.

Red meat is a very important part of most people's diets. The iron that is found in red meat is extremely beneficial to women.

There is a definite difference between beef produced commercially and beef produced naturally.

> By supporting local beef producers we will get the best quality meat to our table

Have you taken a look at the price of ground meat lately? Choosing a ground sirloin over regular ground meat is a better choice and just a little more in price. Choosing a lean roast over ground meat often costs the same.

For the most part there is no traceability and responsibility if something goes wrong with the ground meat that we are buying in the grocery stores today. This does not apply to all grocery store chains, however. There are as many as five different cow scraps from five different farms, sometimes from outside the country.

Sourcing your beef locally means that you are getting the best quality you can trust. There are fewer concerns when you buy and support locally made beef and beef products You know where your food is coming from!

Beef

know your beef

Hockley chipotle chili on chive mash

PREP

Serves 4-6 (plus next day's lunch)
Prep time: 10 minutes
Cooking time: Approx. 30 minutes

INGREDIENTS

CHIVE MASH

large red potatoes	8
sunflower oil	¼ cup
rice milk	splash
chives	¼ cup

CHILI

large Spanish onion, chopped	1 large
sunflower oil	for frying
garlic cloves, chopped	4
ground sirloin	450 grams
thyme sprigs	4
smokey paprika chipotle	4-6 tsps
ground cumin	1 tsp
garlic powder	1 tsp
PC® chipotle hot sauce	14-16 drops
sea salt	to taste
pepper	to taste
red kidney beans	2 - 540ml cans
diced tomatoes	1 - 796ml can
Hockley stout	½ can
tomato paste	½ - 1 can
brown sugar	¼ cup
dried bay leaves	2

TOOLS

1 large stock pot for chili
1 medium pot for potatoes

TIPS

Anyone can make a great chili! Try adding the beans towards the end, they will retain their shape and look absoluetly fresh and taste great!

CHIVE MASH

Peel and boil potatoes in salted water until soft and ready to mash. Add sunflower oil and a splash of rice milk when mashing. Chop up the chives and stir in just before serving.

CHILI

Fry the onion in sunflower oil for a few minutes, then add chopped garlic.

Toss in the ground sirloin and fry only until it browns. Add spices and chipotle hot sauce directly onto the meat and simmer for a few minutes.

Add the kidney beans and tomatoes along with the Hockley beer, tomato paste and brown sugar. Toss in your bay leaves and simmer for about 25 minutes, or until desired thickness.

Your potatoes should be done and ready for mashing before the chili is done.

Serve the chili plated as shown in image directly on the chive mash!

“Chili is delicious and perfect for those winter evenings; a hearty and protein-packed dish that everyone loves.”

Rosemary roasted quail on brown Canadian wild rice

PREP

Serves a family of 4-6
Prep time: 5-10 minutes
Cooking time: Approx. 30-40 minutes

INGREDIENTS

quail	6-12
fresh garlic cloves	6 whole
rosemary	4 sprigs
local beer or wine	1 can
sunflower oil	drizzle
Canadian wild rice	1½ cups
garlic cloves	2 chopped
garlic powder	sprinkle
sea salt and pepper	to taste

TOOLS

1 ceramic roaster with lid
1 pot for rice
1 frying pan

TIPS

Make sure when roasting quail, you roast them in a closed dish to keep in the moisture and retain the great flavour. The kids really love these!

Preheat oven to 350°F.

Wash the quails, removing any stray feathers. Tie their legs and lay them in a ceramic roaster that is small so they are crowded.

Toss in 4 whole cloves of garlic, skin and all, and the 4 sprigs of rosemary. Drizzle a little oil over top, and sprinkle seasonings over all of the birds.

Pour in the beer at the edge of the roaster, so as not to disturb the spices.

Cook uncovered for 15 minutes.

Cover with the lid and cook for 15-30 minutes more. While they are cooking, see below to prepare your rice.

When the quails are done, you may uncover them to brown them up a little under the broiler for a few minutes. Use the drippings to pour over the quail before serving.

RICE

Boil 2½ to 3 cups of water and sea salt.

Add the long grain brown Canadian wild rice. Gently boil for 30 minutes and remove from heat.

Let sit for 15 minutes, or until desired tenderness, and then drain the water.

Sauté the remaining chopped garlic clove for a few minutes, add the wild rice, and sauté for a few more minutes, just enough to get the garlic flavour infused into the rice.

“These little birds cook up best when crammed into a small baking dish. They turn out moist & tender. Using a good local beer adds to their excellent taste.”

Curried whole wheat pasta with chickpeas and baby 'bellas

PREP

Serves 4-6
Prep time: 5 minutes
Cooking time: Approx. 20-25 minutes

INGREDIENTS

whole wheat pasta	375 grams
baby bellas	227 grams sliced
sunflower oil	for frying
sea salt	to taste
fresh ground pepper	to taste
curry	1-2 tsp
paprika	1-2 tsp
garlic powder	1-2 tsp
scallions	3 chopped
chickpeas	1 can rinsed

TOOLS

1 large pot
1 large frying pan
colander
small bowl
serving bowl

TIPS

With this recipe as the base, you can add chopped zucchini, baby tomatoes, and any kind of beans. Keeping an eye on what is in season makes it a year-round recipe that can be changed to suit what is available. Nothing wrong with including chicken or beef strips to add extra protein.

Château des Charmes Estate Bottled Sauvignon Gris,
VQA Niagara-on-the-Lake

Sauv Gris Gewurztraminer
Andert Wines Austria,
Wunsch Mann Alsace France, Calamus Niagara

Start by boiling salted water for the pasta. Once immersed, it takes up to 8 minutes for good quality pasta to cook.

Clean and cut the mushrooms into quarters. Fry them in sunflower oil on high heat, seasoning lightly with sea salt and pepper.

Mix the other seasonings in a bowl ahead of time, so you can add them gradually to the pasta, allowing you to adjust the taste slowly.

Rinse the chickpeas under cool water, chop the scallions, and set both aside.

Once the pasta is cooked, drain and put it into a serving bowl. Toss in the chickpeas and fried mushrooms. Season to your taste with the mixed spices.

Drizzle in as much oil as you like and finish off with the chopped scallions.

Simple, fresh and easy!

“This pasta was created with having fun in mind. Simple and care free dishes are often some of the greatest creations. Have fun with your food!”

Lavender, chocolate and edible flowers

While travelling through the Niagara Region I came across a wonderful couple who grows lavender as a sustainable crop.

The operation, Busy Bee Gardens (Lavender Grower), is owned and operated by Robert and Melissa Ashal who are celebrating their first year in the business of lavender production.

I was excited to travel into the Niagara Region, have a visit and pick up some more wonderful products. Not only do they carry lavender and its essential oil, they also carry other fine essential oils and edible flowers.

This is a really nice place to visit as they are in the process of producing essential oils from the lavender crops. Their store is full of wonderful natural therapeutic essential oils of all kinds, as well as soaps, creams and massage oils. They have invested in a pharmaceutical grade glass-blown distiller to produce the essential oils on site.

They took us on a tour of their facility introducing us to lemon grass and other essential oil-producing plants.

Robert and Melissa believe that nature has what we need right in our own backyard. Both of them are very passionate about what they are doing and feel that using natural essential plant oils can be very effective in relieving headaches, is good for the skin and scalp, and is used to help those having difficulty sleeping at night. It has a very relaxing effect overall and smells quite wonderful.

I bought fresh lavender to use in my baking along with some other edible flowers and some really nice lemon grass spray. The lavender is fantastic with chocolate and cookie recipes. We use the lemon grass spray to freshen up the room form time to time, and because it is natural and not chemically based, we feel quite comfortable about using it around the kids.

Invest in a lavender flower-filled pillow as a natural sleep aid

These types of products have a very unique place in the market, since many of us are looking to use more natural and safe products that require no prescriptions and that have no harmful side effects.

From my own personal experiences, I also know that the lavender plant itself attracts bees. This is a very positive, as bees need flowers to produce, pollinate and sustain.

Seek out wonderful little places like this, you not only get to experience something new but learn a lot along the way.

Try lavender in your cookies, muffins and cakes, and if your having trouble relaxing, invest in a lavender flower-filled pillow as a natural sleep aid.

Lavender
is essential

Decadent chocolate lavender cake

PREP

Serves a family of 4-6
Prep time: 10 minutes
Baking time: None!
Refrigeration time: Approx. 4 hours

INGREDIENTS

Green & Black's Organic® 65% orange and spice chocolate	2 bars
non-hydrogenated lard	½ cup
maple syrup	¼ cup
egg	1 large
graham crackers	6 broken
walnut halves	½ cup
dried cranberries	½ cup
golden raisins	½ cup
dried lavender flowers	3-4 sprigs
Amaretto®	splash

TOOLS

1 pot
1 frying pan
1 small bowl
1 mixing bowl
3 x 8 loaf pan
parchment paper

TIPS

Sourcing local chocolate is definitely a challenge. This chocolate contains no dairy, but may contain traces of milk ingredients, so be careful when purchasing chocolate for those who are allergic.
Really the best chocolate is a high quality chocolate.

Château des Charmes Estate Bottled Cabernet Franc Icewine, VQA Niagara-on-the-Lake

Icewine Sauternes, Barsac, Riesling Auslese

Loaf pan must be lined with parchment paper for easy removal.

Melt the lard together with the maple syrup over medium heat. Remove from heat to low and melt in the chocolate bars, stirring until creamy.

Add the beaten egg and stir it in completely. Make sure the chocolate mixture is warm, not at cooking temperature. Set aside.

Put the walnuts into a frying pan on high heat and toast them a little. Turn off the heat for 30 seconds, then pour in a generous splash of Amaretto®.

Turn the element on low and simmer for a few minutes, then on high to reduce the liqueur until no more liquid exists and the nuts are caramelized with a sugary coating.

Put the caramelized walnuts, cranberries, raisins, lavender flowers and broken graham crackers into a bowl, leaving some cranberries and lavender out for topping.

Stir in the chocolate mixture and then pour it all into the parchment lined pan. Decorate the top with cranberries and lavender and refrigerate for 4 to 4½ hours.

Parchment paper makes it easy to remove from the pan—also great trick for brownies and sticky cake recipes. Slice and serve.

To make it totally awesome, coat your serving plate with dark chocolate an hour before you're ready to serve, then drizzle over the slices with melted light chocolate and sprinkle with lavender for a beautiful presentation.

How decadent is that?

“Simply delicious chocolate. No butter, no milk, yet creamy and full of flavour. Who says great tasting chocolate comes from a brown cow?”

Mini-bran cakes with toasted sunflower seeds, wild blueberries and dates

PREP

Makes 8 mini cakes
Prep time: 10 minutes
Baking time: Approx. 30-35 minutes

INGREDIENTS

raw unsalted sunflower seeds	¼ cup
whole wheat flour	1 cup
all-purpose flour	1 cup
pure orange extract	1 tsp
baking powder	1 tsp
baking soda	1 tsp
sea salt	½ tsp
bran	1 cup
shredded coconut	1 cup
sunflower oil	½ cup
dark brown/cane sugar	1 cup
egg	1 egg
unsweetened applesauce	½ cup
vanilla	1 tsp vanilla
molasses	¼ cup
cranberry juice	½ cup
dates	8
wild blueberries	1 cup

TOOLS

2 bowls
1 frying pan
1 large loaf pan or suare muffin pan (8)

TIPS

Your sunflower seeds must be raw and preferably organic. Roasted sunflower seeds have been soaked in oil and will destroy your bran cakes. So read the package carefully to make sure you're getting the right ones!

Preheat oven to 375°F.

Toast sunflower seeds for 3-4 minutes in a frying pan and let cool.

Combine all of the dry ingredients in a bowl and set aside.

Cream together the sunflower oil and sugar, until creamy.

Add the egg and the applesauce and keep blending.

Next add the vanilla, molasses and cranberry juice. All the dry ingredients can then be added to the liquid mixture with the coconut.

Once everything is completely mixed, stir in the toasted sunflower seeds.

Pour the batter into the loaf pan and set the dates on the surface.

Bake for about 30-35 minutes on the middle rack. The edges should start to get brown when it is cooked.

This is a bran cake you will want to eat and enjoy with your family anytime!

“These are my killer bran cakes. With some local fruit and seeds, some fresh dates, they are delicious for breakfast or a light snack! Does anyone know of a local date farmer who wants to go on a date?”

Cran-apple bran muffins

PREP

Makes 12 medium muffins
Prep time: 5 minutes
Baking time: Approximately 35-40 minutes

INGREDIENTS

Empire apple	1 grated
whole wheat flour	1 cup
all-purpose flour	1 cup
baking powder	1 tsp
baking soda	1 tsp
cinnamon	2 tsp
ginger	1 tsp
all spice	1 tsp
sunflower oil	¾ cup
brown sugar	¾ cup
eggs	2
maple extract	1 tsp
apple juice	1 cup
maple syrup	¼ cup
crushed bran	2 cups
dried cranberries	½ cup

TOOLS

tray(s) for 12 muffins
mixer
2 large bowls

TIPS

Try using grated carrots, pears and zucchini. All will bake up quite nicely using this recipe as a base. You could even use fresh cherries, chopped apricots and local peaches—the muffin possibilities are endless.

Preheat oven to 350°F.

Start by peeling and grating the apple. Set aside.

Mix all your dry ingredients in a bowl and set aside. In another large bowl, mix the oil, brown sugar and eggs until creamy.

Add the liquids gradually, alternating with the flour mixture. Once this is completely mixed, add the bran and finally the cranberries and the grated apple.

Pour the mixture right up to the tops of oil sprayed muffin trays. This will give you really nice muffin tops - the crunchiest part that everyone enjoys!

Bake in the oven at 350°F for 35-40 minutes.

Cool on a wire rack and enjoy!

“If you love muffins that have a crunchy top and are light and tasty, try this one. I made it just for you!”

Baked pears with fall spices and blueberry brandy reduction

PREP

Serves a family of 4-6
Prep time: 5-10 minutes
Baking time: Approx. 1 hour

INGREDIENTS

BAKED PEARS

pears in season	6 whole
apple juice	2 cups
water	1 cup
Disaronno®	¼ cup
whole cloves	½ cup
cinnamon sticks	2 sticks
allspice	sprinkle
brown sugar	2-4 tbsp

BLUEBERRY REDUCTION

fresh local blueberries	1 quart
cane or brown sugar	2 tbsp
blueberry brandy	a few splashes!
cornstarch	1-2 tsp

TOOLS

1 pot
11 x 15 ceramic baking dish
foil

TIPS

Try using distinctive liqueurs when cooking fruits. The alcohol is cooked off and the flavour left behind is amazing. Cloves, cinnamon and other spices really kick up the dish!

Preheat oven to 425˚F.

BAKED PEARS

Wash the pears and place them in the ceramic baking dish. Add the whole cloves and cinnamon sticks. Sprinkle on the allspice and brown sugar. Add the apple juice and water.

In a frying pan, cook your Disaronno to burn off the alcohol. Drizzle over the pears and cover the baking dish with foil.Bake for about 1 hour.

Keep an eye on the liquid; add more as it cooks down.

For fully cooked pears, bake until you get the appearance you want. There are no hard and fast rules when cooking fruits and vegetables.

They can be on the firm side or cooked soft —try them both ways!

Optional, image served without.

BLUEBERRY REDUCTION

Rinse and cook down the blueberries in the pot with either cane or brown sugar, until they look a little soft and turn a beautiful deep purple.

Add blueberry brandy liqueur and reduce until the sauce is the desired consistency.

Reducing the liquid makes the sauce thicken and the flavour is more intense!

Thicken with 1-2 tsp of cornstarch.

Set aside to drizzle over the cooked pears just before serving.

“Baking local fall fruits is simple, fun and delicious! Coating the pears with sticky sweetness makes them irresistable.”

Apple pecan salty cardamom shortbread envelopes

PREP

Makes 18 cookies
Prep time: 10-15 minutes
Baking time: 20-25 minutes

INGREDIENTS

Salty cardomom shortbread dough
recipe on next page

organic Delicious apples	1-2 chopped
brown sugar	1 tsp
lemon juice	2 tsp
cinnamon	1 cup
apple juice or water	¼ cup
amaretto	splash

TOPPING

pecans	¾ cup
amaretto	¼ cup chopped

DRIZZLE

maple syrup	½ cup
brown sugar	½ cup

TOOLS

1 bowl
3 frying pans
hand-held blender
rolling pin
2 sheets parchment paper
2¼ inch square cookie cutter
2 baking sheets

TIPS

To make this an all-season cookie, you can easily substitute apples, blueberries, strawberries, red currants and more. Check the in-season directory, and spice it up with local in-season fruit.

Preheat oven to 335˚F.

THE COOKIES
Between 2 sheets of parchment paper, roll out the dough to about ¼ inch thick. (For old cookie sheets, also use parchment paper for baking for brown bottoms.)

Cut 2¼ inch squares, until all the cookies are cut and ready for filling. Holding a square in one hand, pinch the middle of each side so the 4 corners stand up, looking like an open envelope or box (see photo).

Place on a baking sheet. Make your applesauce while cookies are baking in the oven. Just before they are ready for filling, carmelize your pecans.

Once all the cookie shells are on baking sheets, spoon in the apple cinnamon filling. Bake for 20-25 minutes on the middle rack. Sometimes a pinched side will open while baking, this is how they got their name, one side open looks like an open envelope!

You can drizzle them immediately out of the oven. As the maple syrup cools in the cookie, it turns into a firm candy-like, yummy good part of the cookie!

APPLESAUCE
Turn the stove element to high, put the chopped apples in the frying pan with the brown sugar, apple juice, lemon juice and cinnamon. Turn down to medium and cook for about 5 minutes.

CONTINUED ON PAGE 361

“I love salty and sweet. There is something about this taste that plays on your senses. These cookies are a great treat for the kids, but they could also be served with a nice dessert wine at a dinner party.”

Salty cardamom shortbread dough

PREP

Makes one dough recipe
Prep time: Approx. 10 minutes

INGREDIENTS

whole wheat flour	1¼ cup
all-purpose flour	1¼ cup
sea salt	1½ tsp
cardamom	2 tsp
ground cloves	2 tsp
pure vanilla extract	1 tsp
icing sugar	½ cup
non-hydrogenated lard	1 cup plus 4 tbsp

TOOLS

mixer
plastic wrap

TIPS

When making this recipe, if your dough is a little crumbly, add a tablespoon or two while in the mixer until it has the consistency of a soft dough. Otherwise it will not hold together to make the cookies. If there is too much shortening, the cookies will be oily and will not cook properly.

Combine the dry ingredients, including spices, but not the icing sugar, and set aside.

Cream the lard with the icing sugar and vanilla extract. I personally like almond extract. Then slowly mix in the dry ingredients until completely mixed into soft dough.

Lay ball on enough plastic wrap to cover it completely, press the dough flat, about 1½ inch thick, and wrap tightly.

Dough can be stored in the refrigerator for up to 3 days, or frozen for a couple of weeks.

If using some immediately, place it in the refrigerator for 45 minutes to 1 hour first. To use it from the fridge, warm it for 60 seconds in the microwave before rolling it in between two sheets of parchment paper. This makes it really easy to work with.

Each batch can make up to 24 cookies, one European tart, or one pie shell.

Apple pecan salty cardamom shortbread envelopes cont'd

CONTINUED FROM PAGE 358

Put half of the apple mixture back into the bowl, leaving the other half in the frying pan and, and turn off the stove.

Blend the portion in the bowl, adding the amaretto, until it looks like applesauce. Return the contents of the bowl to the frying pan and mix with the apples.

Turn the element to low heat and reduce for 3-4 minutes, until no juice is left and the mixture is thick and bubbling. Turn it off and let it cool.

PECANS
Toast the chopped pecans in a hot pan and remove from the element for 2 minutes. Add the amaretto, return to the heat, and reduce until the nuts are sticky and no liquid remains. Set aside to cool.

MAPLE SYRUP DRIZZLE
It is important to only prepare this once the cookies are almost cooked or are cooling.

Put the frying pan on high heat, and reduce the maple syrup and brown sugar until the sugar dissolves. Cook down until it thickens a little and starts to bubble.

At this point it is ready to drizzle. It will start to firm up once it starts to cool. After adding the pecans, spoon the reduction onto each cookie, letting it drizzle down the sides. Cool completely and serve.

The kids will love these! You will too!

Maple lemon jalapeño cornbread muffins

PREP

Makes 6 large muffins
Prep time: 5 minutes
Baking time: Approx. 20-25 minutes

INGREDIENTS

sunflower oil	¼ cup
large egg	1
cane or brown sugar	½ cup
whole wheat flour	¾ cup
all-purpose flour	¾ cup
#120 cornmeal (very coarse)	1 cup
baking powder	2 tsp
baking soda	1 tsp
sea salt	½ tsp
fresh lemon juice	4 tbsp
rice milk (add 2 tbsp of oil)	1 cup
lemon zest	2 tsp

JALAPEÑO REDUCTION

green jalapeño peppers	2 finely chopped
maple syrup	¼ to ½ cup

TOOLS

frying pan
2 bowls
mixer
large 6 muffin tray
bamboo skewer stick

TIPS

Creating a corn muffin that has amazing texture is what I was looking for. Using a very coarse cornmeal definitely adds to the crunchiness. You can sub in a finer one if you like, but you will miss out on the crunch!

Preheat oven to 350°F.

Clean out the seeds and cut the jalapeños into small pieces. In the frying pan, on high, cook them down in the maple syrup until they are sticky coated.

You will get a great hot taste with a sweet sensation if you reduce them like this.
Set aside.

In your mixer, cream together the sunflower oil, egg and sugar, for about 5 minutes or until creamy in texture.

Combine all the dry ingredients in a separate bowl while the mixer is going.

Add the dry ingredients to the creamy mix, alternating with the lemon juice and rice milk, until everything is completely mixed. Now add the lemon zest.

Pour the batter equally into greased muffin tins, up to ¾ full. Drizzle the jalapeño reduction into each muffin.

Stir each one with a bamboo skewer stick to make sure the jalapeño pieces do not all stick together.

Top up the muffins with the rest of the batter. Bake for 20 - 25 minutes, or until brown on top.

Cool on a rack for about 10 minutes.

“I decided that, by applying some Spanish influence and a little maple syrup, I could come up with a tasty corn muffin with a hot, sweet pepper tucked inside. Jalapeños make this muffin.”

Now the muffins are gone, let's make some more!

This book is alive because Anastasia inspired me to document how we have taken on the dairy-free challenge we were faced with. We both thought we might be able to help others living similar lives to ours. I feel it has become increasingly important to share my healthy lifestyle with you, incorporating dairy-free recipes.

Because of her food allergies, I have learned to be diligent in reading all labels, and I have had to change our eating habits in order to protect the safety of our daughter. I have to admit, this was one of the most difficult challenges I have ever had to face. Through living and eating differently, I have been awakened to many other lifestyle changes that I can make that have helped me and my family adapt.

I started to recognize what food actually contains today, and figured out that there is a definite connection between all things I have talked about in this cookbook.

What we have found over the years is that our family and friends are loving how we cook, and how we incorporate local and in season foods into our everyday diet. Eating the way we do, we have found that our energy levels are higher and we feel good about the conscious choices we make every day. We are connected to our food.

Eating healthy is not about deciding to adopt a lifestyle change that is strict and impossible for you. It's about living a lifestyle that you can blend into a daily routine and make it part of your life—for the rest of your life. Many people tend to jump on and off the band wagon of yo-yo dieting and dietary changes, thinking that it's a quick fix. However, the reality is that dietary changes need to be permanent. Personal commitments have to be strong and consistent.

I wanted to help stimulate similar thoughts within you so you could see what I see. The globalization that has happened around food is not necessarily a positive move for anyone. Your local community should come first, keeping your local choices as close to home as possible. This keeps local famers working, for you and me.

I believe in healthy, dairy-free eating, reading food labels and local in season cooking. I have been inspired and I hope I have inspired you!

Slow down a little, enjoy life and eat well.

Stacey Fokas

Websites

www.freshalicious™.ca

Contributors

www.cowhide.ca
www.berettaorganics.com
www.busybeegardens.com
www.cherryavenuefarms.org
www.chateaudescharmes.com
www.eatlocalcaledon.org
www.everdale.org
www.feastforthepalate.com
www.hockleybeer.ca
www.pingueprosciutto.com
www.silvercreekponds.com
www.slwr.com
www.stonemillbakehouse.com
www.windyfieldsmushrooms.blogspot.com
www.wholecirclefarm.ca

Allergy Info

www.anaphalaxis.ca
www.anaphalaxis.org
www.allergicliving.ca